EASY GENIUS
SCIENCE PROJECTS

with

Electricity and Magnetism

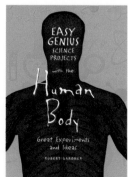
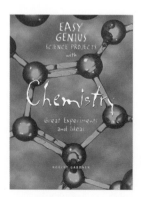

EASY GENIUS
SCIENCE PROJECTS
with

Electricity and Magnetism

Great Experiments and Ideas

Robert Gardner

Enslow Publishers, Inc.
40 Industrial Road
Box 398
Berkeley Heights, NJ 07922
USA
http://www.enslow.com

Library of Congress Cataloging-in-Publication Data

Gardner, Robert, 1929–
    Easy genius science projects with electricity and magnetism : great experiments
        and ideas / Robert Gardner.
        p. cm. — (Easy genius science projects)
    Summary: "Science projects and experiments about electricity and magnetism"—
        Provided by publisher.
    Includes bibliographical references and index.
    ISBN-13: 978-0-7660-2923-1
    ISBN-10: 0-7660-2923-9
    1. Electricity—Experiments—Juvenile literature. 2. Magnetism—Experiments—
        Juvenile literature. 3. Science projects—Juvenile literature. I. Title.
    QC527.2.G377 2009
    537.078—dc22
                                                        2007038470

Printed in the United States of America

10 9 8 7 6 5 4 3 2 1

To Our Readers: We have done our best to make sure all Internet Addresses in this book
were active and appropriate when we went to press. However, the author and the publish-
er have no control over and assume no liability for the material available on those Internet
sites or on other Web sites they may link to. Any comments or suggestions can be sent by
e-mail to comments@enslow.com or to the address on the back cover.

♻ Enslow Publishers, Inc., is committed to printing our books on recycled paper. The paper
in every book contains 10% to 30% post-consumer waste (PCW). The cover board on the
outside of each book contains 100% PCW. Our goal is to do our part to help young people
and the environment too!

Illustration Credits: © 2008 by Stephen Rountree (www.rountreegraphics.com), Figures
1–21; © bubaone/iStockphoto.com, trophy icons; © Chen Fu Soh/iStockphoto.com, back-
grounds.

Photo Credits: © David H. Lewis/iStockphoto.com, p. 46; © Don Bayley/iStockphoto.com,
p. 82; © Jo-Hanna Wienert/iStockphoto.com, p. 12; Shutterstock, pp. 26, 102, 117.

Cover Illustration: Shutterstock

CONTENTS

CHAPTER 1

Electricity: A First Look with Early Scientists
13

CHAPTER 2

Magnetism: A First Look with Early Scientists
27

CHAPTER 3

Electric Cells, Batteries, Circuits, Currents, Volts, and Amps
47

◐ *Indicates experiments that offer ideas for science fair projects.*

Electricity and Magnetism: A Connection 83

Faraday, Electric Motors, and Generators 103

⊘ *Indicates experiments that offer ideas for science fair projects.*

INTRODUCTION

Electricity and magnetism are a part of physics, which deals with matter and energy. By doing the experiments in this book, you will find that electricity and magnetism are closely linked. Together they provide the energy needed to light our homes and run the many appliances, such as refrigerators, toasters, computers, televisions, and cell phones, that we use every day. Without electricity and magnetism, our lives would be very different.

As you carry out the activities in this book, you may need a partner to help you. It would be best if you work with someone who enjoys experimenting as much as you do. In that way, you will both enjoy what you are doing. **If any safety issues or dangers are involved in doing an experiment, they will be indicated. In some cases, to avoid danger, you will be asked to work with an adult. Please do so.** We do not want you to take any chances that could lead to an injury.

Like any good scientist, you will find it useful to record your ideas, notes, data, and anything you can conclude from your investigations in a notebook. By doing so, you can keep track of the information you gather and the conclusions you reach. It will allow you to refer back to things you have done and help you in doing other projects in the future.

Science Fairs

Some of the investigations in this book contain ideas you might use at a science fair. These projects are indicated with a symbol (⊙). However, judges at science fairs do not reward projects or experiments that are simply copied from a book. For example, a diagram of the magnetic field around a bar magnet would not impress most judges. Finding a unique way to measure the magnetic force at different distances from a magnetic pole would be more likely to attract their attention.

Science fair judges tend to reward creative thought and imagination. It is difficult to be creative or imaginative unless you are really interested in your project. Choose an investigation that appeals to you. Before you jump into a project, you should consider your own talents and the cost of the materials you will need.

If you decide to use an experiment or idea found in this book for a science fair, find ways to modify or extend it. This should not be difficult because you will discover that as you carry out investigations new ideas come to mind. Ideas will come to you that could make excellent science fair projects, particularly because the ideas are your own and are interesting to you.

If you decide to enter a science fair and have never done so, you should read some of the books listed in the Further Reading section. These books deal specifically with science fairs. They provide plenty of helpful hints and useful information that will help you to avoid the pitfalls that sometimes plague first-time entrants. You will learn how to prepare appealing reports that include charts and graphs, how to set up and display your work, how to present your project, and how to relate to judges and visitors.

Safety First

Safety is essential when you do experiments. Your eyes require particular protection. They can be damaged by chemicals or flying fragments. The likelihood of an injury is very small because most of the projects included in this book are perfectly safe. However, read the following safety rules before you start any project.

1. Do any experiments or projects, whether from this book or of your own design, **under the adult supervision** of a science teacher or other knowledgeable adult.

2. Read all instructions carefully before doing a project. If you have questions, check with your supervisor before going any further.

3. Maintain a serious attitude while conducting experiments. Fooling around can be dangerous to you and to others.

4. **Always wear safety goggles** when doing experiments that could cause particles to enter your eyes.

5. Do not eat or drink while experimenting.

6. Have a first aid kit nearby while you are experimenting.

7. Never let water droplets come in contact with a hot light bulb.

8. Never experiment with household electricity. Instead, use batteries.

9. Use only alcohol-based thermometers. Older thermometers may contain mercury, which is a dangerous substance.

10. Always wear shoes, not sandals, while experimenting.

Your Notebook

Your notebook, as any scientist will tell you, is a valuable possession. It should contain ideas you may have as you experiment, sketches you draw, calculations you make, and hypotheses you may suggest. It should include the data you record, such as voltages, currents, resistors, weights, and so on. It should also contain the results of your experiments, calculations, graphs you draw, and any conclusions you may be able to reach based on your results.

THE SCIENTIFIC METHOD

Scientists look at the world and try to understand how things work. They make careful observations and conduct research. Different areas of science use different approaches. Depending on the problem, one method is likely to be better than another. Designing a new medicine for heart disease, studying the spread of an invasive plant, such as purple loosestrife, and finding evidence of water on Mars all require different methods.

Despite the differences, all scientists use a similar general approach in doing experiments. This is called the scientific method. In most experiments, some or all of the following steps are used: observing a problem, formulating a question, making a hypothesis (an answer to the question), making a prediction (an if-then statement), designing and conducting an experiment, analyzing results, drawing conclusions, and accepting or rejecting the hypothesis. Scientists then share their findings by writing articles that are published.

You might wonder how to start an experiment. When you observe something, you may become curious and ask a question. Your question, which could arise from an earlier experiment or from reading, may be answered by a well-designed investigation. Once you have a question, you can make a hypothesis. Your hypothesis is a possible answer to the question. Once you have a hypothesis, it is time to design an experiment to test a consequence of your hypothesis.

In most cases, you should do a controlled experiment. This means having two groups that are treated the same except for the one factor being tested. That factor is called a variable.

For example, suppose your question is "Do green plants need light?" Your hypothesis might be that they do need light. To test the hypothesis, you would use two groups of green plants. One group is called the control group; the other is called the experimental group. The two groups should be treated the same except for one factor. Both should be planted in the same amount and type of soil, given the same amount of water, kept at the same temperature, and so forth. The control group would be placed in the dark. The experimental group would be put in the light. Light is the variable. It is the only difference between the two groups.

During the experiment, you would collect data. For example, you might measure the plants' growth in centimeters, count the number of living and dead leaves, and note the color and condition of the leaves. By comparing the data collected from the control and experimental groups over a few weeks, you would draw conclusions. Healthier growth and survival rates of plants grown in light would allow you to conclude that green plants need light.

Two other terms are often used in scientific experiments—dependent and independent variables. One dependent variable in this example is healthy growth, which depends on light being present. Light is the independent variable. It does not depend on anything.

After the data are collected, they are analyzed to see if they support or reject the hypothesis. The results of one experiment often lead you to a related question. Or they may send you off in a different direction. Whatever the results, something can be learned from every experiment.

Lightning is similar to static electricity.

Chapter 1

Electricity: A First Look with Early Scientists

KNOWLEDGE ABOUT ELECTRICITY probably began with Thales (640–546 B.C.) of Miletus. Thales was an early Greek philosopher. He discovered that a piece of amber (a hard, colorful fossil resin) would attract many small objects after being rubbed with a cloth.

William Gilbert (1544–1603) was an English scientist. He was probably the first to investigate electricity by doing experiments. He did not simply develop theories to explain observations. He did experiments to test theories.

The experiments in this chapter **must be done in dry air.** Dry air (low humidity) is most common in the winter. Cold air is quite dry.

Things you will need:

- puffed rice cereal or a small piece of a foam packing peanut
- thread
- tape
- plastic comb
- thin aluminum foil
- plastic ruler
- cloth
- drinking straw
- push pin
- lump of clay

In dry air, you can do experiments similar to those done by Gilbert. Electricity is the study of charged particles. Static electricity is the study of charges that are not moving.

1. Hang a piece of puffed rice cereal or a small piece of a foam packing peanut from a long thread. Rub a plastic comb on your clothing. Bring it near the puffed rice or foam (Figure 1a). What happens?

   After a short time, the cereal or foam is repelled by (moves away from) the comb. Why do you think that happens?

2. Gilbert built a *versorium*, which means "turn around" in Latin. You can build your own versorium. Use a ruler to find the exact center of a drinking straw. Push the sharp end of a push pin through the exact center of the straw. Use a thicker pin or a tack to widen the hole.

3. Set the base of the push pin in a lump of clay (Figure 1b). Put the straw on the push pin. Be sure the hole is wide enough so the straw can turn freely. Gilbert used his versorium to see which things would attract the versorium when rubbed with a cloth. You can do the same.

Electricity

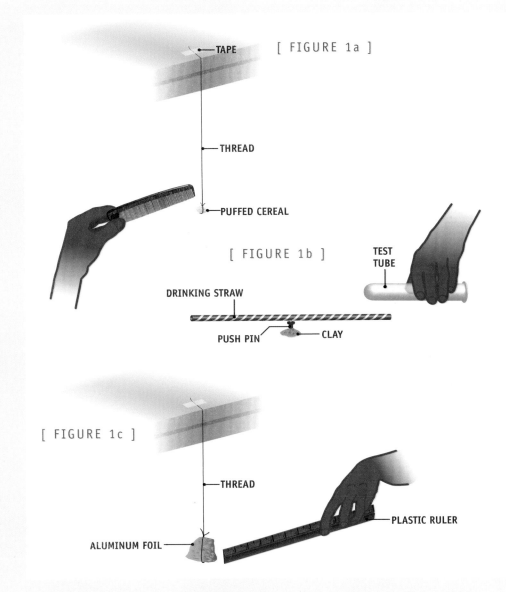

[FIGURE 1a]

TAPE

THREAD

PUFFED CEREAL

[FIGURE 1b]

TEST TUBE

DRINKING STRAW

PUSH PIN — CLAY

[FIGURE 1c]

THREAD

PLASTIC RULER

ALUMINUM FOIL

Experiments with electricity in dry air. 1a) Charge a comb by rubbing it with a cloth. Hold it near a piece of puffed cereal or a packing peanut. b) Make a versorium and use it to test for static charge. c) What happens when charges collect on a piece of aluminum foil?

4. Rub a comb with a cloth. Bring it near one end of the versorium. Does the versorium move? Does a glass object, such as a test tube, rubbed with silk attract the versorium? How about a large iron nail rubbed with a cloth? What happens if you hold the versorium near a TV screen? What does the result tell you?

5. Hang a small piece of aluminum foil from a thread (Figure 1c). Rub a plastic ruler briskly with a cloth. Bring the ruler near the aluminum. What happens? What do you predict will happen after a short time? Were you right?

   Gilbert tried to explain the attractions you have seen. He said that an invisible electric fluid exists in some kinds of matter. Rubbing removes some of the fluid. As the fluid "flows" back, it carries other bits of matter with it. But why would objects repel one another? Gilbert had no answer.

1.2 Benjamin Franklin and Static Electricity

Things you will need:
- 2 plastic rulers
- thread
- woolen cloth
- glass test tube or glass rod
- silk cloth

Benjamin Franklin (1706–1790), one of the United States' founding fathers, was also an accomplished scientist. He was best known for flying a kite in a thunderstorm to show that lightning is similar to static electricity. He was also very lucky. Several who tried to repeat his experiment were killed by the lightning.

Like Gilbert, Franklin believed that electricity was an invisible fluid. However, he did explain why objects might repel as well as attract. He knew that objects can become electrically charged by rubbing. He hung a glass rod from a thread. He rubbed the rod with a wool cloth. He said the wool gained a lot of electric fluid from the glass. The glass then had less electric fluid. Objects with lots of electric fluid, he said, were positively charged. Objects with little electric fluid were negatively charged.

He brought the wool near the glass rod. They attracted (moved toward) one another. The wool had gained a lot of electric fluid. The glass had lost electric fluid. From experiments like this, he concluded that objects with an opposite charge attract. Other experiments showed him that objects with the same charge repel (push away) one another.

1. Suspend a plastic ruler from a thread. Rub the ruler briskly with a woolen cloth. According to Franklin, the cloth may have

taken electric fluid from the ruler. If it did, what will happen when you bring the woolen cloth near the suspended ruler? Try it. Was Franklin right?

2. What will happen if we bring objects with like charges near one another? Rub a second plastic ruler with the same woolen cloth. Rub the suspended ruler again with the woolen cloth. Both rulers are charged in the same way. What do you predict will happen when you bring the second ruler close to the first one? Try it! Were you right?

   There was no way Franklin could know whether an object was positively charged (had lots of electric fluid) or negatively charged (had little electric fluid). He decided to call the charge on a glass rod rubbed with silk "positive" charge. A rubber rod rubbed with fur attracted a glass rod rubbed with silk. Therefore, he defined "negative" charge as the charge found on a rubber rod rubbed with fur. His definition of positive (+) and negative (–) charge is still used today.

3. Is the charge on the suspended ruler you rubbed with a woolen cloth positive or negative? To find out, rub a glass test tube or a glass rod with a silk cloth. Remember the charge on glass rubbed with silk is positive.

   Bring the glass near a suspended plastic ruler you have rubbed with wool. What happens? Does the ruler have a positive or a negative charge? How can you tell?

4. Remove two strips of clear plastic tape, each about 15 cm (6 in) long, from a roll. Fold a short length at each end of both strips to make a tab you can grasp. Hold the two strips near one another. Is there a force between them? If so, is it an attractive or a repelling force?

Place the sticky side of one strip on the non-sticky side of the other. Hold the strips by their tabs and pull them apart. What happens when you slowly bring the two strips near one another? How do the charges on the two strips compare? Is the charge the same or different? How can you tell? Determine whether the charge on each strip is positive or negative.

 Ideas for a Science Fair Project

- Repeat Experiment 1.1 using different materials and different cloths. For example, try charging various plastic and wooden objects, balloons, and other things with paper towels, rayon, and nylon as well as woolen and silk cloths. Bring each charged object near the charged suspended ruler. What do you find? How many kinds of charge are revealed by this experiment?

- Do an experiment to see how the force between two charged objects is related to the distance between them.

- Sprinkle some salt crystals on a dark sheet of paper. Charge a balloon by rubbing it with a cloth. Hold the balloon over the crystals. Slowly lower the balloon toward the crystals. What happens? Can you explain what you observe?

1.3 Inducing Charge

In Experiment 1.1 the puffed cereal was attracted to the comb, but you had not charged the cereal. Why was it attracted? Let's see if other things can be attracted.

1. Tear a sheet of paper into tiny pieces. Charge a plastic ruler by rubbing it with a woolen cloth or a paper towel. Bring the charged ruler close to the pieces of paper. Is the paper attracted to the ruler?

2. Blow some bubbles using a bubble wand and some bubble-making solution. Bring a charged plastic ruler near the falling bubbles. What happens?

3. Charge the ruler again. Hold the ruler near a very thin stream of water flowing from a faucet. What happens to the stream of water?

Apparently any of these uncharged items are attracted to a charged object. To explain these results, we assume that matter is filled with electric charges. An object with a positive charge has more positive charges than negative charges. An object with a negative charge has more negative charges than positive charges. The electrical attractions you saw are explained by what is called induction.

Suppose the ruler was negatively charged. When you brought it near the paper, the negative charges in the paper were repelled by the negative charges on the ruler. The positive charges in the paper were attracted to the ruler. As a result, the positive charges were closer to the negatively charged ruler than were the negative charges. Electrical forces decrease with distance. Therefore, the positive parts of the paper were more strongly attracted than the negative parts were repelled. A similar thing happened when you brought the charged ruler near the bubbles.

The stream of water was attracted to the ruler for a somewhat different reason. One side of a water molecule has a slight negative charge. The other side has a slight positive charge. Such molecules are said to be polar. If the ruler carried a negative charge, the positive sides of the water molecules were attracted to the ruler. The attractive force between the ruler and the molecules made the stream move toward the ruler. Of course, the negative sides of the molecules were repelled by the ruler. But the molecules turned so that the positive ends were closer to the ruler than were the negative ends. Therefore, the attractive force was greater than the repelling force. As a result, the water moved toward the ruler.

4. Show that either a positively or negatively charged object will attract a water stream.

Things you will need:
- wide-mouth jar or drinking glass
- cardboard
- pencil
- scissors
- paper clip
- aluminum foil
- thin aluminum foil
- plastic ruler
- woolen cloth or paper towel

Electroscopes can detect electric charge. They can also tell whether an object is charged positively (+) or negatively (−). You can build a simple electroscope.

1. Put the open side of a wide-mouth jar or drinking glass on a sheet of cardboard. Use a pencil to outline the mouth of the jar or glass on the cardboard. **Ask an adult** to cut out the cardboard circle.

2. Unfold a paper clip into an "L" shape (Figure 2a). Use the long end of the paper clip to make a hole in the center of the cardboard circle.

3. Crumple a 30-cm (12-in) square of aluminum foil into a ball. Stick it on the long end of the paper clip as shown.

4. Use scissors to cut a strip 8 cm × 0.5 cm (3 in × 0.25 in) from a piece of thin aluminum foil. Fold the strip in half. Hang it on the "L" as shown in Figure 2a. The two sides of the strip are the electroscope's "leaves."

Electroscope

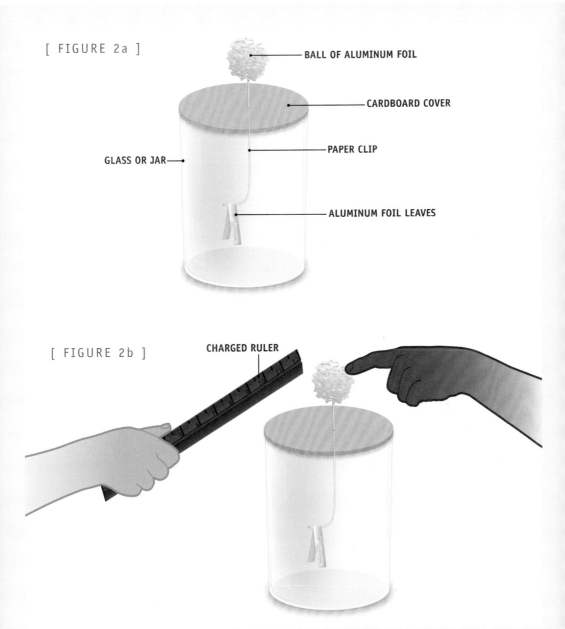

[FIGURE 2a]

BALL OF ALUMINUM FOIL

CARDBOARD COVER

PAPER CLIP

GLASS OR JAR

ALUMINUM FOIL LEAVES

[FIGURE 2b]

CHARGED RULER

2a) You can make an electroscope. b) Ground an electroscope with a charged ruler nearby.

5. Put the cardboard circle on top of the jar or glass. Tape it in place. The electroscope is ready for use.

6. Rub a plastic ruler with a wool cloth or a paper towel. Slowly bring the ruler near the aluminum ball without touching it. What happens to the electroscope's leaves? Can you explain what happened? How does the charge on the leaves compare with the charge on the plastic ruler?

7. Charge the ruler again. Hold it in one hand away from the electroscope. Place a finger of your other hand on the aluminum ball at the top of the electroscope. See Figure 2b. This grounds the electroscope. It allows charges to flow through your body to the earth (ground). Bring the charged

Ideas for a Science Fair Project

- Build a variety of electroscopes. Explain how they are alike and how they differ.

- Use static electricity to make paper cutouts dance, and a paper wheel or a Ping-Pong ball roll along a table, or make a paper strip electroscope, an electric swing, and other static electric toys.

ruler near (but not touching) the top of the electroscope. Then remove your finger from the ball. Next, move the ruler away from the ball. What happens to the leaves? Use what you know about induction to explain what you observed.

8. Very slowly bring the ruler toward the aluminum ball again. What happens to the leaves? What does this tell you about the charge on the leaves? Are the charges on the ruler the same or opposite those on the leaves? How do you know?

This photo shows the pattern of a magnetic field around a bar magnet.

Chapter 2

Magnetism: A First Look with Early Scientists

ACCORDING TO LEGEND, magnets are named for Magnes. Magnes was an ancient Greek shepherd. He noticed that particles of lodestone stuck to his iron crook. Lodestone (magnetite), a compound of iron and oxygen, is magnetic. It attracts iron and some other metals. Since ancient times, small pieces of lodestone were used as compass needles to help sailors navigate.

Thales of Miletus was the first to investigate which rocks were attracted to lodestone. Then Petrus Peregrinus, in the thirteenth century, described what he had learned about magnets. He explained their polarity and how to identify north and south poles. William Gilbert, whom you met in Chapter 1, was the first to do extensive experiments with magnets. He wrote a book entitled *De Magnete* ("Concerning Magnets"). You can do experiments similar to his.

2.1 Magnets, Compasses, and

Things you will need:

-thread

-tape

-bar magnets, or square or circular ceramic magnets

-toothpick

-marking pen and tape

-magnetic compass

-square or circular ceramic magnets with holes in their centers

-soda straw

1. Use a compass to find magnetic north in the area where you are experimenting.

2. Using thread and tape, hang a bar magnet or a square or circular ceramic magnet. Wait for the magnet to stop turning. Its north pole (or one flat side if square or round) will point or be turned in a northerly direction. If it is not, there are other magnetic materials nearby. Move the magnet to a point far from any metals.

3. If the magnet is not marked, mark an "N" on the end or side that is northernmost. Mark an "S" on the other end or side.

4. Repeat the experiment with a second magnet. If not marked, mark it as you did the first magnet.

     The ends or sides of the magnets that you have marked N or S are called poles. The pole marked N is the magnet's north-seeking pole. The pole marked S is its south-seeking pole.

Poles

5. Bring the north-seeking pole of one magnet near the north-seeking pole of a second magnet. What happens?

6. Bring the north-seeking pole of one magnet near the south-seeking pole of a second magnet. What happens?

7. Bring the south-seeking pole of one magnet near the south-seeking pole of a second magnet. What do you think will happen? Try it! Were you right?

   What can you conclude about the force between like poles of magnets? Is it an attractive or a repelling force? How about the force between opposite poles?

8. Slowly bring the north-seeking pole of a magnet near the north-seeking pole of a compass needle. What do you think will happen? Try it! Were you right?

   What do you think will happen if you slowly bring the south-seeking pole of a magnet near the north-seeking pole of a compass needle?

9. Obtain several square or circular ceramic magnets with holes in their centers. See if you can make these magnets "float" above one another on a soda straw.

Ideas for a Science Fair Project

- Make a magnet from a nail. Stroke the entire length of the nail with a bar magnet. Apply all strokes in the same direction with the same pole of the magnet. After about thirty strokes, test the nail to see if it behaves like a magnet.

- Investigate ways to remove the magnetic properties of the magnet you made.

- Make a simple compass like ones used by ancient sailors. Make a sewing needle into a magnet. Remove the bottom from a foam cup. Put the foam bottom in a bowl of water. Place the needle on the foam. Can you identify the magnet's north-seeking pole?

- Make a variety of magnetic compasses from ordinary materials you can find in your home or school.

2.2 Magnets, Magnetic Matter, and Nonmagnetic Matter

Things you will need:

-3 file cards

-flat square or round ceramic magnet

-large steel washer

-thick cardboard

-scissors

-tape

-marking pen

-a friend

-magnetic compass

-various objects such as another magnet, coins, paper, nails, copper wire, iron wire, aluminum foil, plastic and glass objects, chalk, brass objects, rubber bands or erasers, wooden pencils, paper clips, and other common objects

-thread

-bar magnet

Gilbert's experiments led him to divide matter into three types: magnets, magnetic matter, and nonmagnetic matter. A true magnet both attracts and repels another magnet. Magnetic matter can be magnetized, but is not a magnet itself. It will be attracted to either pole of a magnet. Once the attracting magnet is removed, the matter will not behave like a magnet. Finally, nonmagnetic matter is neither attracted nor repelled by a magnet.

1. Prepare some mystery cards. Place three file cards side by side. On one, place a flat square or round ceramic magnet. On the second, place a large steel washer. On the third, place a square piece of thick cardboard about the same size as the magnet.

2. Fold each card in half. Tape the edges together so the objects inside cannot be seen. Label the cards A, B, and C.

3. Ask a friend to test each card by bringing it near each pole of a magnetic compass. Can your friend decide which card contains a magnet?

4. Have your friend cover the labels with tape while you are not watching. Can you identify what is in each card? What is different about the way the compass responds to the washer and the magnet?

5. Gather a variety of objects and a magnet. You might include another magnet, coins, paper, nails, copper wire, iron wire, aluminum foil, plastic and glass objects, chalk, brass, rubber bands or erasers, wooden pencils, paper clips, and other common objects.

6. Use tape and thread to suspend a magnet. Then bring the objects near the magnet.

   Divide the objects into three groups: (1) things that attract one pole of the magnet and repel the other pole; (2) things that attract both poles of the magnet; (3) things that have no effect on either pole of the magnet.

   What kinds of objects are in each group? Do all metals attract the magnet? If an object attracts the magnet, does that necessarily mean the object is a magnet?

7. Classify the materials you tested into things that are magnets, magnetic matter, and nonmagnetic matter.

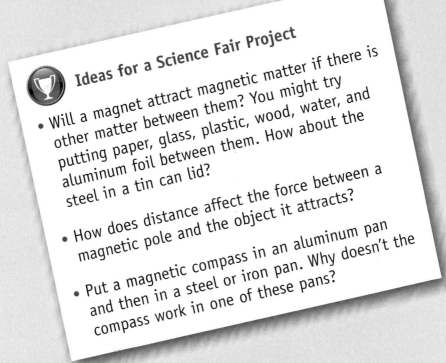

Ideas for a Science Fair Project

- Will a magnet attract magnetic matter if there is other matter between them? You might try putting paper, glass, plastic, wood, water, and aluminum foil between them. How about the steel in a tin can lid?

- How does distance affect the force between a magnetic pole and the object it attracts?

- Put a magnetic compass in an aluminum pan and then in a steel or iron pan. Why doesn't the compass work in one of these pans?

2.3 Our Magnetic Earth

Things you will need:
- cardboard
- bar magnet or a stack of ceramic magnets
- magnetic compass
- map of western hemisphere showing North and South America and north and south poles

William Gilbert was the first to suggest that Earth behaves like a giant magnet. He used a magnetite sphere to make a model of Earth. By moving a compass over the sphere, he showed that the compass behaved just as it does on Earth's surface. You can make a similar model.

1. Cut a circle about 15 cm (6 in) in diameter from a sheet of cardboard. The cardboard can represent a cross-section of Earth. (See Figure 3.)

2. Place a bar magnet or a stack of ceramic magnets along the model's diameter as shown. Notice that the magnet's poles are not in line with Earth's north and south poles.

3. Move a magnetic compass along the model's surface. Move it from its geographic South Pole to its geographic North Pole. What happens to the compass needle as you move it?

4. Use your model, a map, and a compass to answer the following questions. Suppose you took a compass to the Boothia

Peninsula, north of Hudson Bay in northern Canada. Boothia is about 1,200 miles from Earth's geographic North Pole. There, at about 76 degrees latitude, 100 degrees west longitude, you would find Earth's south-seeking magnetic pole. Why is it a south-seeking magnetic pole? In what direction would a compass needle point if you were directly above Earth's

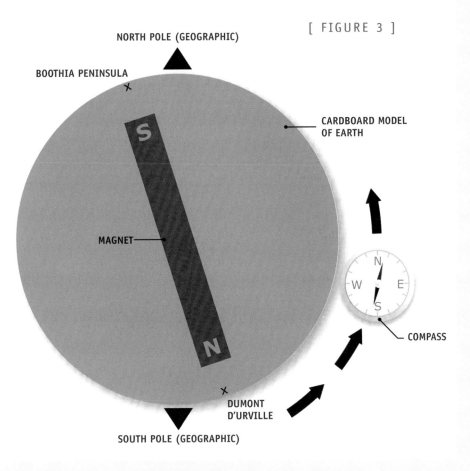

[FIGURE 3]

NORTH POLE (GEOGRAPHIC)

BOOTHIA PENINSULA

CARDBOARD MODEL OF EARTH

MAGNET

COMPASS

DUMONT D'URVILLE

SOUTH POLE (GEOGRAPHIC)

A model of our magnetic Earth.

south-seeking magnetic pole? In what direction would a compass needle point if you were over Earth's north-seeking pole? That pole is in Antarctica near Dumont d'Urville, about 1,200 miles from Earth's geographic South Pole. It is at 67 degrees latitude and 140 degrees east longitude. (See page 119 for answers.)

Earth's magnetic and geographic poles are in different places. Therefore, compass needles seldom point toward geographic north. Within a degree, the North Star is directly above our North Pole. At night, a compass needle is not likely to point in the direction of the North Star. For example, a compass near Boston, Massachusetts, will point about 15 degrees west of geographic north. A compass near San Diego, California, will point about 15 degrees east of north. There are places where a compass needle does really point north. Such a region lies along the Georgia–South Carolina border.

The angular difference between geographic north and magnetic north is called the magnetic declination. However, Earth's magnetism is constantly changing. Therefore, maps showing magnetic declination have to be revised frequently.

2.4 Make a Magnet or Two

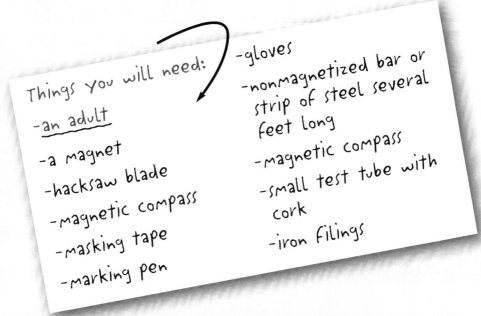

Things you will need:

- an adult
- a magnet
- hacksaw blade
- magnetic compass
- masking tape
- marking pen
- gloves
- nonmagnetized bar or strip of steel several feet long
- magnetic compass
- small test tube with cork
- iron filings

William Gilbert made magnets and compass needles by stroking strips of iron with lodestone (magnetite). You, too, can make a magnet.

1. Use a magnet to stroke a hacksaw blade. Stroke the blade about thirty times. Always stroke in the same direction using the same pole of the magnet as shown in Figure 4a.

2. Bring a compass needle near each end of the hacksaw blade. Which end is the north-seeking pole? Which end is the south-seeking pole?

3. Use tape and a marking pen to label the poles of the magnet you made.

4. **Ask an adult** to put on heavy gloves and break the hacksaw blade in half (Figure 4b). Do you now have two magnets?

5. To find out, bring a compass needle near each end of both halves of the hacksaw blade. Do both halves of the hacksaw

[FIGURE 4a]

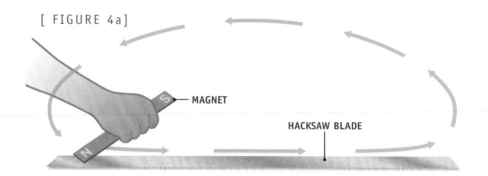

MAGNET

HACKSAW BLADE

[FIGURE 4b]

N   ? ?   S

COMPASS

HAMMER

[FIGURE 4c]

STEEL BAR

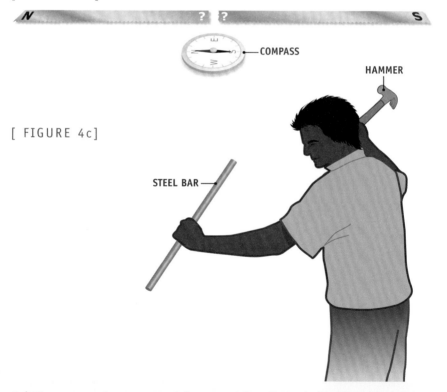

4a) You can make a magnet from a strip of steel. b) If you break a
magnet in half, will there be poles at the broken ends? c) Make
a magnet out of a steel bar.

blade now each have their own north- and south-seeking poles?

Like you, Gilbert discovered that breaking a magnet in half results in two new poles at the broken ends.

By experimenting, Gilbert discovered that he could change an iron bar into a magnet by hitting it. You can duplicate his experiment.

6. Find a bar or strip of steel several feet long that has not been magnetized. To make sure it is not already a magnet, hold each end near a compass needle. If it is already magnetized, one end will attract the north-seeking pole of the compass. It will repel the south-seeking pole. If it is a magnet, try dropping it on a hard surface a few times. This should erase its magnetism. If not, look for another bar or strip. Then test it again.

7. Hold the bar along a north-south line parallel to the direction of a compass needle. Then turn it downward so it dips about 70 degrees (Figure 4c). Hit it several times with a hammer.

8. Test again with a compass to see if the bar has become a magnet.

9. Fill a small test tube with iron filings. Put a cork in the tube. Stroke the test tube with one pole of a magnet. Carefully pick up the test tube in a horizontal position. Hold it close to a magnetic compass. Has the tube of filings become a magnet?

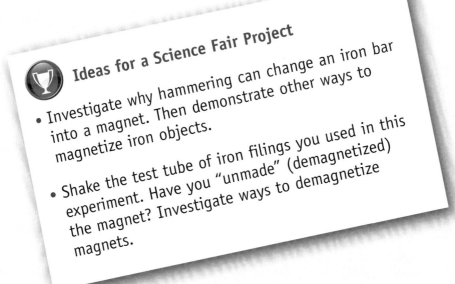

Ideas for a Science Fair Project

- Investigate why hammering can change an iron bar into a magnet. Then demonstrate other ways to magnetize iron objects.

- Shake the test tube of iron filings you used in this experiment. Have you "unmade" (demagnetized) the magnet? Investigate ways to demagnetize magnets.

2.5 Magnetic Dip

Things You will need:

- tape
- round toothpick
- hacksaw blade
- two glasses
- strong magnet
- magnetic compass

Gilbert noticed that a magnetic compass not only pointed north, it dipped. A compass needle also dipped on his model. In fact, it dipped straight down when it was above the model's south-seeking pole. The dipping compass was further evidence that Earth behaves like a giant magnet.

To show that a magnet dips you must first have a balanced nonmagnetized strip of metal.

1. Tape a round toothpick to the center of a nonmagnetized hacksaw blade. Place the ends of the toothpick on two identical glasses as shown in Figure 5a.

2. If the blade is not balanced (level), add a small piece of clay to the side that is uppermost. Move the clay along the blade until it balances.

3. Remove the blade. Place it toothpick-side down as shown in Figure 5b. Stroke it about thirty times with a strong magnet to make the blade into a magnet.

4. Use a compass to determine which end of the blade is the north-seeking pole. Replace the toothpick on the glasses. Be sure the north-seeking end of the blade is northernmost. Notice that the north-seeking end of the blade now dips down.

The farther north a compass needle moves, the more it dips. Near central Florida, it dips about 60 degrees. Near central Michigan, it dips about 75 degrees. In Boothia Peninsula, Canada, it dips 90 degrees. How would it turn near Earth's north-seeking pole in Antarctica? (See page 119 for the answer.)

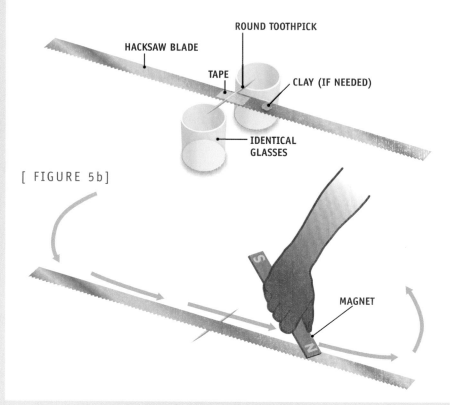

[FIGURE 5a]

ROUND TOOTHPICK

HACKSAW BLADE

TAPE

CLAY (IF NEEDED)

IDENTICAL GLASSES

[FIGURE 5b]

MAGNET

5a) Balance a hacksaw blade on two glasses. Use a toothpick as a fulcrum. Add a piece of clay if necessary to make it balance.
b) Magnetize the blade by stroking it with a strong magnet. Then put it back on the two glasses.

🏆 2.6 A Magnetic Field

Things you will need:
- bar magnet
- wooden table or floor
- sheet of white cardboard about 30 cm (12 in) square or a sheet of white paper taped to cardboard
- iron filings (borrow from school or make by filing steel nails or by cutting steel wool into very short lengths)
- one or more magnetic compasses
- paper
- pencil

Michael Faraday (1791–1867) was a great English scientist. He introduced the idea that there are fields of force around magnets and electric charges. We cannot see these fields, but Faraday discovered a way to map them. You can map a magnetic field in the same way Faraday did.

1. Place a bar magnet on a wooden table or floor. Place a sheet of white cardboard on the magnet.

2. Sprinkle iron filings on the cardboard. Tap the cardboard gently with your finger. You will see a pattern emerge.

   Faraday was a visual thinker with no mathematical training. To him, the pattern of filings revealed magnetic lines of force. Together the lines of magnetic force make the magnetic field around the magnet visible. The filings "feel" the magnetic force and line up in the direction of the force at

[FIGURE 6]

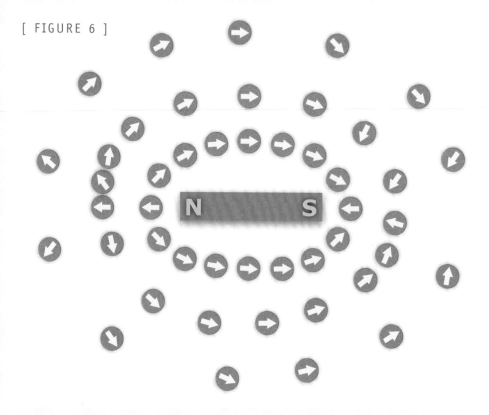

The pattern of magnetic lines of force around a bar magnet can be mapped by many magnetic compasses.

each point. The magnetic force is greatest where the lines are close together.

3. You can also map the field around a bar magnet with a compass or compasses. Place the magnet on a sheet of paper. Put the compass or compasses at various places around the magnet. Draw a little arrow just in front of the north-seeking pole of the needle. This is the direction of the field. Draw a dash just behind the south-seeking end of the compass needle.

After you do this a number of times, you will see the magnetic field pattern emerge. Figure 6 shows a field revealed by many small compasses around a bar magnet. Is it similar to the one you drew?

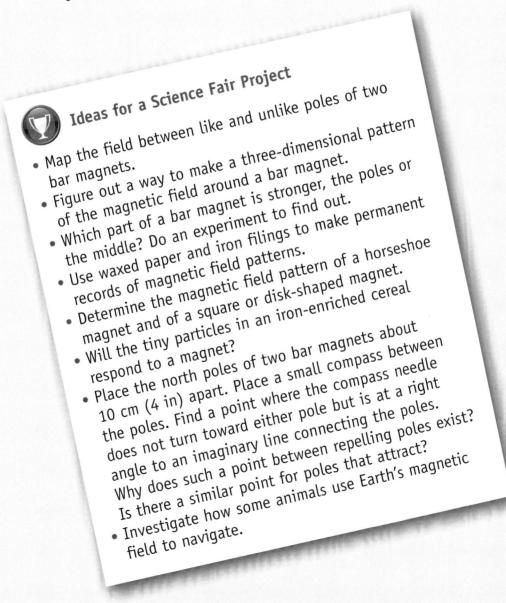

Ideas for a Science Fair Project

- Map the field between like and unlike poles of two bar magnets.
- Figure out a way to make a three-dimensional pattern of the magnetic field around a bar magnet.
- Which part of a bar magnet is stronger, the poles or the middle? Do an experiment to find out.
- Use waxed paper and iron filings to make permanent records of magnetic field patterns.
- Determine the magnetic field pattern of a horseshoe magnet and of a square or disk-shaped magnet.
- Will the tiny particles in an iron-enriched cereal respond to a magnet?
- Place the north poles of two bar magnets about 10 cm (4 in) apart. Place a small compass between the poles. Find a point where the compass needle does not turn toward either pole but is at a right angle to an imaginary line connecting the poles. Why does such a point between repelling poles exist? Is there a similar point for poles that attract?
- Investigate how some animals use Earth's magnetic field to navigate.

A car battery works in the same way Volta's voltaic pile did: Two different metals generate current through an acid.

Chapter 3

Electric Cells, Batteries, Circuits, Currents, Volts, and Amps

DURING THE EIGHTEENTH CENTURY, scientists found ways to generate large amounts of static electricity. Luigi Galvani (1737–1798), professor of anatomy at the University of Bologna, had a static charge generating machine in his laboratory. He noticed that the muscles of dissected frogs twitched when struck by a spark of charge. Muscles would also twitch when touched by two different metals. Galvani believed the electricity came from the muscle. He called it animal electricity.

Alessandro Volta (1745–1827), an Italian physicist, had a different idea. He believed the electricity was caused by touching the moist flesh with two different metals. His idea led to the invention of the world's first battery.

A buildup of static charge can cause a sudden discharge— a spark or, in nature, lightning. Volta's battery provided a steady flow of charge along a wire. Charge flowing along a wire is called an electric current.

You can make a battery similar to one Volta made. It is called a voltaic pile. You can measure its voltage (energy per charge) with a voltmeter. The electric current it generates can be measured with an ammeter. An ammeter measures electric current (number of charges per second) in units called amperes (A). Microamperes (μA) are millionths of an ampere; milliamperes (mA) are thousandths of an ampere.

3.1 Volta's Battery: A Voltaic Pile

Things you will need:
- 6 pennies and 6 dimes
- paper towel
- scissors
- lemon juice
- two insulated wires with ends such as alligator clips to make connections
- voltmeter*
- microammeter*

* Arbor Scientific (see Appendix) sells an inexpensive combination ammeter and voltmeter that will measure currents in four stages from 0 μA to 5 A and voltage from 0 mV to 50 V.

1. You can make an electric cell. Begin by cutting a strip of paper towel slightly wider than a penny. Cut a square from one end of the strip. Place the square on a penny. Add a drop of lemon juice to the square. Put a dime on top of the wet paper square.

2. Place the penny-paper-dime "sandwich" on an alligator clip connected to a wire leading to one pole of a voltmeter (Figure 7a). Press the dime firmly with the alligator clip of a wire connected to the other pole of the voltmeter. If the voltmeter gives a positive reading, the connections are correct. If the meter moves to the left (to a negative reading), reverse the connections. The voltmeter's poles are labeled plus (+) and minus (−). Is the dime or the penny connected to the positive pole of the voltmeter? The coin connected to the positive pole of the voltmeter is the positive electrode of the battery. What is the voltage across the electric cell?

4. Connect the electric cell to an ammeter that can read current in microamperes. What current is generated by the cell?

[FIGURE 7a]

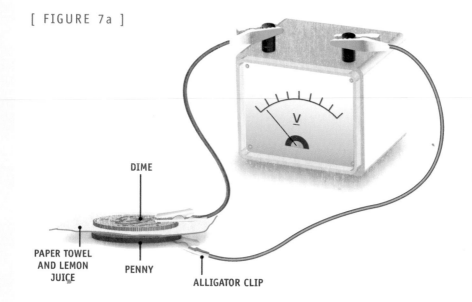

DIME

PAPER TOWEL
AND LEMON
JUICE

PENNY

ALLIGATOR CLIP

[FIGURE 7b]

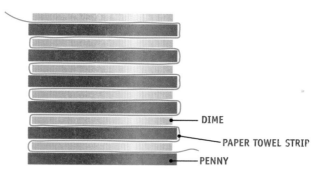

DIME

PAPER TOWEL STRIP

PENNY

7a) An electric cell can be made from a penny, a dime, and a piece
of paper towel soaked with lemon juice. b) A series of cells
make up a battery or voltaic pile.

5. Make a battery (voltaic pile) from a series of six penny-dime electric cells. Cut a strip from a paper towel. It should be 2.5 cm (1 in) wide and 30 cm (12 in) long. Wet the paper strip with lemon juice. Weave it between a stack of pennies and dimes as shown in Figure 7b. Notice that pennies and dimes alternate. Starting with a penny on the bottom, there should be a dime at the top.

6. What is the voltage of the battery you have made? How much electric current can it generate?

Electric Cells and Batteries

An electric cell consists of two electrodes and an electrolyte. The electrodes are usually two different metals. The electric cell you made in Experiment 3.1 had a penny as one electrode. The other electrode was a dime. Between the electrodes there is an electrolyte. The electrolyte is usually a wet or moist material. It will allow a charge to move through it. You used lemon juice as an electrolyte.

It is tedious to build a voltaic pile every time you need an electric current. It is more convenient to use D-cells as a source of voltage and current. (D-cells are often called batteries. Actually, a battery is two or more electric cells joined together.)

A carbon rod at the center of a D-cell serves as its positive electrode. The carbon rod sits in an electrolyte of powdered carbon mixed with manganese dioxide, ammonium chloride, and water. The entire cell is enclosed in a zinc can. The zinc serves as the negative electrode. By connecting D-cells end to end you can make a battery.

Things you will need:

- an adult

- 4 D-cells
- cardboard mailing tube
  with a diameter
  approximately the same
  diameter as the D-cells
  (about 3.2 cm or 1.25 in)

- shears

- ruler

- aluminum pie pan
- wide rubber band
- connecting wires (2)
- voltmeter that measures
  0-6 volts or more
- pen or pencil
- notebook
- graph paper

A battery is a combination of several electric cells. You can make a 6-volt battery using four D-cells.

1. Place four D-cells next to a cardboard mailing tube that has approximately the same inside diameter as the D-cells (about 3.2 cm or 1.25 in). See Figure 8a.

8a) Place four D-cells head to tail (+ to –). Cut a cardboard mailing tube slightly shorter than the four cells. b) Cut a slot along the length of the tube. c) Place the tabs between the cells and at each end of the battery. Hold the cells together with a wide rubber band. d) Measure the voltage across one, two, three, and all four D-cells. e) Two D-cells are connected in parallel.

Electric Cells

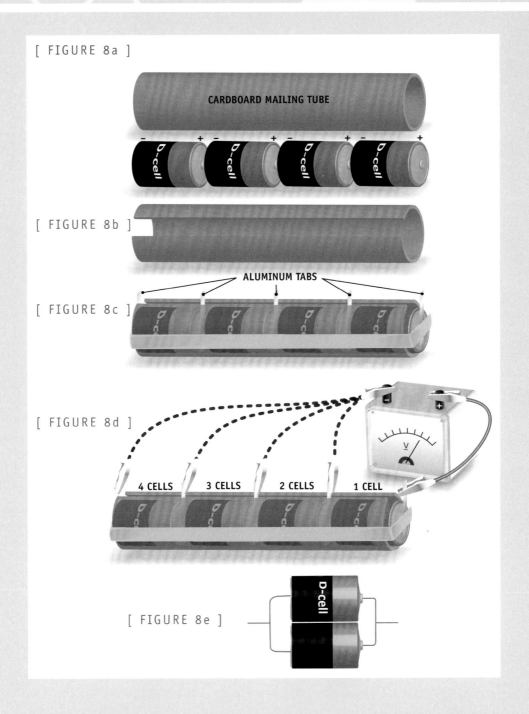

[FIGURE 8a]

CARDBOARD MAILING TUBE

− + − + − + − +
D-cell D-cell D-cell D-cell

[FIGURE 8b]

ALUMINUM TABS

[FIGURE 8c]

D-cell D-cell D-cell D-cell

[FIGURE 8d]

4 CELLS 3 CELLS 2 CELLS 1 CELL

V

[FIGURE 8e]

D-cell

2. **Ask an adult** to cut the mailing tube about 1 cm (0.5 in) shorter than the total length of the four D-cells. **Ask the adult** to also cut a slot 2 cm (0.75 in) wide along the entire length of the tube (Figure 8b).

3. Use shears to cut five pieces of thick aluminum from the thickest part of an aluminum pie pan, which will probably be the rim. The pieces (tabs) should be about 4 cm × 2 cm (1.5 in × 0.75 in). Place them between the cells and at each end of the battery (Figure 8c). The tabs should stick up above the D-cells so they can be connected to wires. Put a wide rubber band around the entire battery. It will hold the cells firmly against the tabs that serve as connecting points.

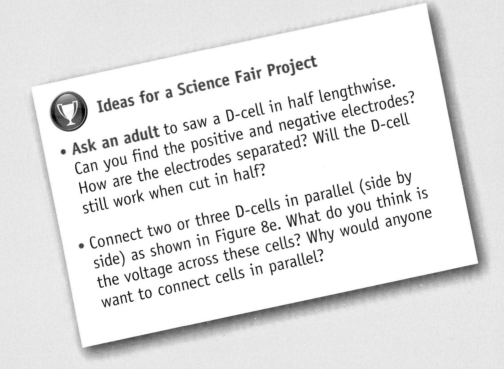

Ideas for a Science Fair Project

- **Ask an adult** to saw a D-cell in half lengthwise. Can you find the positive and negative electrodes? How are the electrodes separated? Will the D-cell still work when cut in half?

- Connect two or three D-cells in parallel (side by side) as shown in Figure 8e. What do you think is the voltage across these cells? Why would anyone want to connect cells in parallel?

4. Connect one, then two, then three, and finally all four D-cells of the battery to a voltmeter that can read at least 6 volts (Figure 8d). Record the voltage for each connection. What is the voltage across one D-cell? Across two D-cells? Across three? Across the entire battery?

5. Plot a graph of voltage versus number of cells. Plot voltage on the vertical axis and number of D-cells on the horizontal axis. What can you conclude from the graph?

Save your 4-D-cell battery for other experiments.

3.3 A Simple Electric Circuit:

Things you will need:

-D-cell

-bare wire about 12 cm (5 in) long or an unfolded paper clip

-flashlight bulb

-figure 9

An electric circuit is a path along which electric charges may travel from one electrode of a battery to the other. If you connect one electrode to the other with a wire, that would be a circuit. However, such a circuit is called a short circuit. It would make the battery very hot. The battery would soon stop working.

In this experiment you will build an electric circuit. The circuit will consist of a D-cell, a wire, and a flashlight bulb.

1. See if you can make the bulb glow using one bare wire (or a paper clip) and a D-cell.

2. Once you succeed, examine Figure 9. Predict which circuits in Figure 9 will light the bulb. Then test your predictions. Do not leave any connected for long because some are short circuits. Which ones are short circuits? (See page 119 for answer.)

Just for Fun

Build a quiz board using a bulb, D-cell, and wires. Write questions on the left side and answers on the right. For example, question: What is 2 × 2?; answers: 2, 4, 6, 8. The person being quizzed tries to connect a wire leading from the question to the correct answer. When the connection to the right answer is made, the bulb lights.

Bulb, Wire, and D-Cell

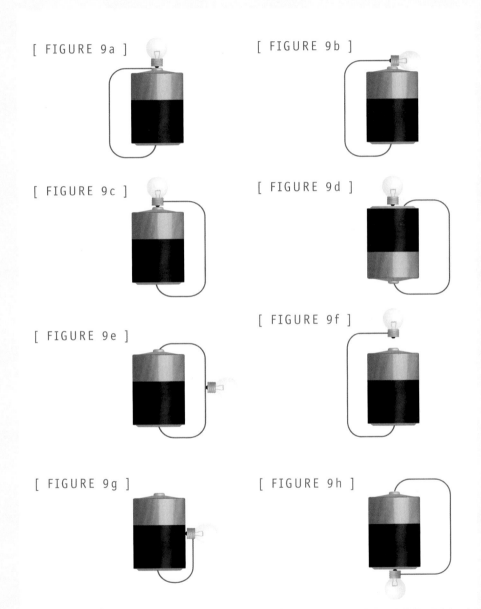

[FIGURE 9a]

[FIGURE 9b]

[FIGURE 9c]

[FIGURE 9d]

[FIGURE 9e]

[FIGURE 9f]

[FIGURE 9g]

[FIGURE 9h]

**In which arrangements will the bulb light? In which arrangements
will it not light? Which arrangements are short circuits?**

3.4 Another Circuit: Bulb, Bulb

Things you will need:

- battery built in Experiment 3.2
- 6.3-volt screw-type bulb
- bulb holder
- insulated wires with connecting clips
- voltmeter that measures 0–6 volts or more
- pen or pencil
- notebook
- ammeter that measures 0–1 amperes or more
- graph paper

Scientists use shorthand when they draw circuits. Figures 10a–f show the symbols used to represent parts of electrical circuits. In many experiments that follow, this shorthand will be used to show you the circuits you will need to build.

1. Build the circuit shown in Figure 10g. Use the battery you built in Experiment 3.2, a bulb, a bulb holder, and insulated wires with connecting clips.

2. Connect a voltmeter across the bulb as shown in Figure 10h. The voltmeter is said to be in parallel with the bulb. The positive pole of the meter should connect to the side of the bulb that is connected to the battery's positive electrode. The negative pole of the meter should connect to the side of the bulb that is connected to the battery's negative electrode.

Holder, Wires, Battery, and Meters

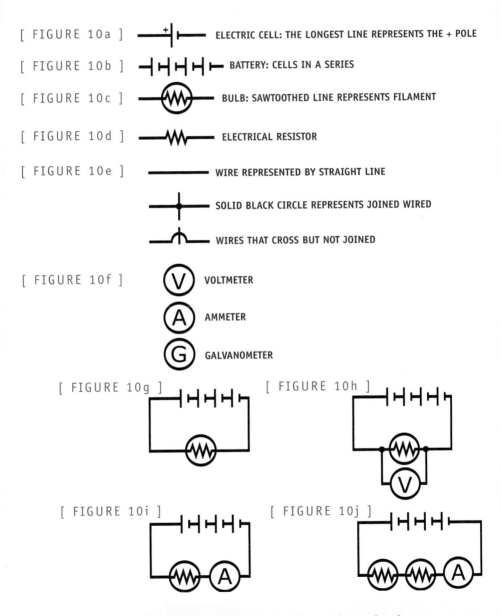

[FIGURE 10a] ELECTRIC CELL: THE LONGEST LINE REPRESENTS THE + POLE

[FIGURE 10b] BATTERY: CELLS IN A SERIES

[FIGURE 10c] BULB: SAWTOOTHED LINE REPRESENTS FILAMENT

[FIGURE 10d] ELECTRICAL RESISTOR

[FIGURE 10e] WIRE REPRESENTED BY STRAIGHT LINE

SOLID BLACK CIRCLE REPRESENTS JOINED WIRED

WIRES THAT CROSS BUT NOT JOINED

[FIGURE 10f] VOLTMETER

AMMETER

GALVANOMETER

[FIGURE 10g]

[FIGURE 10h]

[FIGURE 10i]

[FIGURE 10j]

Electrical shorthand makes it easier to draw circuits.

3. What is the voltmeter reading (voltage) across the bulb when the battery consists of four D-cells? When it consists of three D-cells? Of two D-cells? Of one D-cell?

4. Add an ammeter to the circuit as shown in Figure 10i. The ammeter is in series with the bulb. If you are using a meter that is a combination ammeter and voltmeter, you will have to move the meter. If you are using separate meters, you can leave the voltmeter in place.

5. What is the current in the circuit (ammeter reading) when the battery consists of four D-cells? When the battery consists of three D-cells? Of two D-cells? Of one D-cell?

6. Plot a graph of voltage versus current. Plot voltage, in volts, on the vertical axis. Plot current, in amperes, on the horizontal axis. Does doubling the voltage double the electric current?

7. Move the ammeter to the other side of the bulb. It will then be between the bulb and the positive pole of the battery. Is the electric current the same as it was before? What does this tell you?

8. Add a second bulb to the circuit as shown in Figure 10j. Connect to one, two, three, and then four D-cells. For each connection, look at the bulbs' brightness. How does their brightness compare to the brightness when there was only one bulb? How do the currents compare?

9. Unscrew either bulb. What happens to the other bulb? Why does it happen?

Ideas for a Science Fair Project

- Devise a switch so that you can turn a circuit on or off without having to connect or disconnect the battery.

- Build a flashlight with a switch you can use to turn it on or off.

- Design and build your own bulb holder and battery holder.

- Build a simple circuit with a gap that can be used to measure the steadiness of a person's hand.

Things you will need:
- two 6.3-volt screw-type flashlight bulbs
- 2 bulb holders
- 4-D-cell battery
- insulated wires with connecting clips
- voltmeter that measures 0-6 volts or more
- pen or pencil
- notebook
- ammeter that measures 0-1 ampere or more

As you saw in the previous experiment, the electric current was the same on both sides of the bulb. No charge is used up as it flows around a circuit. As many charges come into the battery on one side as go out on the other.

1. Set up the circuit shown in Figure 11ai. The two bulbs are in series. You can vary the voltage by connecting the circuit to one, two, three, or four D-cells. The ammeter is in series with the bulbs. Therefore, the current through the bulbs and ammeter is the same. The voltmeter is connected across both bulbs. Record the voltage in volts, and the current in amperes when one, two, three, and four D-cells are connected to the circuit.

2. Connect the voltmeter so that it measures the voltage across just one bulb (Figure 11aii). Do this for one, two, three, and four D-cells in series. How do these voltages compare with the voltages across both bulbs?

3. Predict the voltages across the other bulb for one, two, three, and four D-cells in series. Then use the voltmeter to measure them. Were you right?

4. Predict the currents for one, two, three, or four D-cells in series if you move the ammeter to the other side of the bulbs. Then move the ammeter and measure the currents. Were you right?

[FIGURE 11ai]

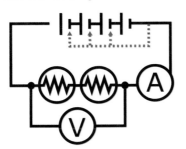

[FIGURE 11aii]

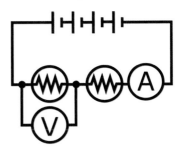

[FIGURE 11bi]

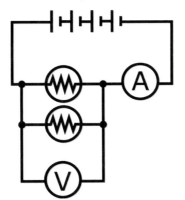

[FIGURE 11bii]

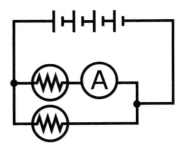

11a) A series circuit (two bulbs in series).
b) A parallel circuit (two bulbs side by side).

5. Arrange the bulbs and meters as shown in Figure 11bi. The bulbs arranged side-by-side like this are said to form a parallel circuit. Measure and record the voltages and currents when the circuit is connected to one, two, three, and four D-cells in series.

6. Change the circuit as shown in Figure 11bii. The ammeter now measures the current through only one bulb. Record the currents when the circuit is connected to one, two, three, and four D-cells. How does the current through one bulb compare with the current that flowed through both bulbs?

7. Predict the current that will flow through the other bulb when the circuit is connected to one, two, three, and four D-cells. Then move the ammeter and measure the currents. Were you right?

Ideas for a Science Fair Project

- Increase the number of bulbs in series until the bulbs no longer glow. Does this mean there is no current in the circuit? How can you find out?

- Build a series circuit using three bulbs that have different voltage ratings. Will the voltage across each bulb be the same? Will the sum of the voltages across each one equal the voltage across all three?

🏆 3.6 A Lemon Cell

Things you will need:

-lemons

-aluminum or galvanized nail

-copper nail

-connecting wires

-microammeter

You can make an electric cell from a lemon. The inside of the lemon will serve as the electrolyte. An aluminum or galvanized nail can be used as a negative electrode. A copper nail will serve as a positive electrode.

1. Squeeze a lemon with your hands to soften it. Stick an aluminum nail or galvanized nail into the lemon. Stick a copper nail into the lemon a short distance from the other nail.

2. Use a wire to connect the aluminum or galvanized nail to the negative pole of a microammeter. Use a second wire to connect the copper nail to the positive pole of the meter. How much current, in microamperes (μA), is generated by the lemon? Can you increase the current by squeezing the lemon? By moving the electrodes?

3. Do you think you can light a flashlight bulb using a lemon cell? Try it. Were you right?

3.7 An LED

A diode is an electronic device that allows electric current to flow in only one direction.

1. Examine a light-emitting diode (LED). Notice that one wire lead is a bit longer than the other.

2. Place two D-cells in series. Hold them together with a wide rubber band.

3. Use an insulated wire to connect the short lead of the diode to the negative pole of the battery. Touch the long lead to the positive pole of the battery. What happens?

4. Reverse the leads. Connect the diode's short lead to the battery's positive pole. Touch the long lead to the negative pole of the battery. What happens this time?

3.8 Electrical Resistance

Things you will need:
- a 10-ohm and a 15-ohm resistor (buy at electronics store)
- medicine cup or a vial
- water
- 4-D-cell battery built in Experiment 3.2
- wires with connectors
- ammeter (0–1 amp)
- voltmeter (0–6 volts)
- pen or pencil
- notebook
- graph paper
- pocket calculator (optional)

Circuit elements such as lightbulbs, electric motors, and resistors "resist" the electric current. They reduce the current flowing through the circuit. Resistors are widely used in electrical appliances to control current and voltage.

1. Place a 10-ohm electrical resistor underwater in a medicine cup or a vial. (We will get to the meaning of *ohm* shortly.) The water will keep the resistor from getting hot. Be sure the resistor stays underwater (Figure 12).

2. Connect the resistor to one D-cell. Use an ammeter and a voltmeter to measure the current through the resistor and the voltage across the resistor. Record your measurements.

3. Repeat the experiment using two, then three, and finally four D-cells. Record current and voltage each time. Use a chart like the one above. It contains the author's results from the same experiment.

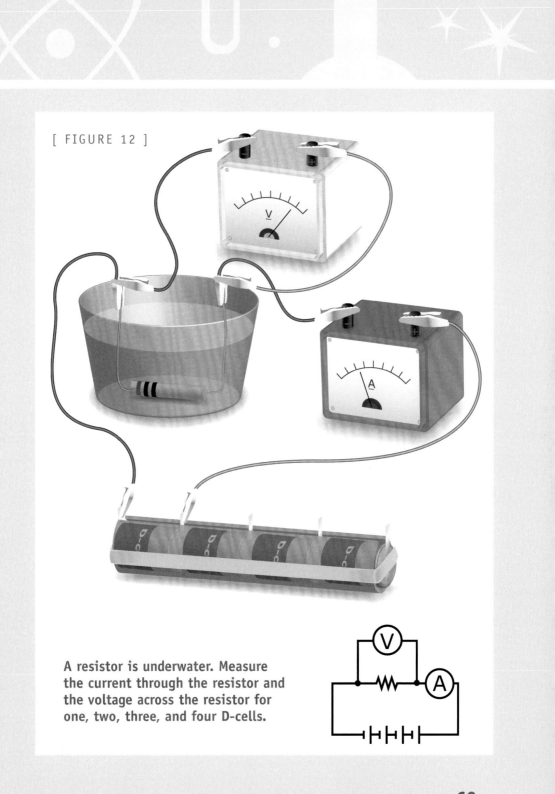

[FIGURE 12]

A resistor is underwater. Measure the current through the resistor and the voltage across the resistor for one, two, three, and four D-cells.

No. of D-cells	Voltage (volts)	Current (amperes)	Voltage/current (volts/amp)
1	1.5	0.15	10.0
2	3.0	0.31	9.7
3	4.6	0.45	10.2
4	5.9	0.60	9.8

4. Use the data you have collected to plot a graph. Plot voltage in volts versus current in amperes. Use a ruler to draw a straight line through the points.

5. Divide the voltage readings by the corresponding current readings. The author's calculations are shown in the last column of the table. How do they compare with yours?

6. Examine the resistor closely. Resistors have colored stripes. The colored stripes are a code that is used to identify the resistor. Each color represents a number. The code is shown on the next page. The first three stripes give the number value of the resistance. A fourth stripe (gold or silver), which you can ignore, indicates how carefully the resistor was made.

   A resistor "resists" the current that the battery tries to push through a circuit. The larger the resistance, the smaller the current.

   Resistance is measured in ohms. 1 ohm is equal to 1 volt divided by 1 ampere, or 1 volt per ampere. 10 ohms is equal to 10 volts per ampere and so on.

   Do your graph and calculations agree with the stripes on your resistor?

color of stripe	number it represents
black	0
brown	1
red	2
orange	3
yellow	4
green	5
blue	6
violet	7
gray	8
white	9

Your resistor stripes were brown-black-black. The first two stripes represent 1 and 0, or 10. The third stripe tells the number of zeroes that follow the first two numbers. In your case, black tells you there are no zeroes after 10. Therefore your resistor is a 10-ohm resistor. If your resistor's stripes were green-violet-red, it would mean it was a 5,700-ohm resistor. What would you call a resistor with red-gray-green stripes?

7. Replace the 10-ohm resistor with a 15-ohm resistor (brown-green-black). Repeat the experiment using the 15-ohm resistor with only the voltmeter connected. Take the ammeter out of the circuit. Try to predict what the ammeter reading will be when you repeat the experiment with the ammeter connected. How closely did your predictions agree with the ammeter readings?

Electrical Resistance and Georg Simon Ohm
Georg Simon Ohm (1787–1854) was a German physicist. He investigated the flow of electric current through wires. Ohm discovered a number of things: (1) current decreases as the length of the wire increases; (2) current increases as the diameter of the wire increases; (3) current flows more easily

through some metals than through others; (4) current decreases as the temperature of the wire increases.

Ohm is best known for a scientific law he discovered. According to Ohm's law, the resistance (R) of a circuit element is the ratio of the voltage (V) across the element to the current (I) flowing through it:

$$resistance = voltage/current, \text{ or } R = V/I.$$

The unit for resistance is named for Ohm. By definition, 1 ohm = 1 volt per ampere.

Examine your data from Experiment 3.4. What was the bulb's resistance when it was connected to one D-cell? To two D-cells? To three D-cells? To four D-cells?

Why do you think the resistance increased as you increased the size of the battery? (See page 119 for an answer.)

3.9 Electrical Resistance and Meters

Things you will need:
- 4-D-cell battery
- 6.3-volt screw-type bulb
- bulb holder
- insulated wires with connecting clips
- voltmeter, 0–6 volts or more
- pen or pencil
- notebook
- ammeter, 0–1 ampere or more

Why do you think an ammeter is placed in series with circuit elements? Why do you think a voltmeter is placed in parallel with circuit elements?
To find out, let's measure the resistance of these meters.

1. Set up the circuit you built in Experiment 3.4 (Figure 10g). Connect the bulb to the 4-cell battery.

2. Put an ammeter in series with the bulb. Put a voltmeter in parallel with the ammeter. What is the current through the ammeter? What is the voltage across the ammeter? What is the resistance of the ammeter, in ohms?

3. Put both a voltmeter and an ammeter in series with the bulb. What is the current through the ammeter, the voltmeter, and the bulb? What is the voltage across the voltmeter? What is the resistance of the voltmeter in ohms?

    What would happen if you put a voltmeter in series with a circuit element? What would happen if you put an ammeter in parallel with a circuit element?

⟨🏆⟩ 3.10 Electrical Resistance

Things you will need:
- pencil lead from a mechanical pencil or wooden pencil and an adult
- insulated wires with clips
- 2-D-cell battery
- 2.3-volt flashlight bulb
- bulb holder
- paper clip
- battery
- ammeter
- voltmeter
- graph paper
- pen or pencil

You may have used a dimmer switch (also called a rheostat). It allows you to control the brightness of a lightbulb by turning a knob. This experiment will show you how a rheostat works.

1. Obtain a pencil lead (graphite) used in mechanical pencils.

2. Place a 2.3-volt flashlight bulb in a bulb holder. Use an insulated wire with clips to connect one side of the bulb holder to one pole of a 2-D-cell battery. Use a second insulated wire to connect the other side of the bulb holder to one end of the pencil lead (Figure 13a).

3. Use a third wire to connect the other pole of the battery to an opened paper clip. Use the paper clip to firmly touch the pencil lead at different places along its length. How does the length of the pencil lead in the circuit affect the brightness of the bulb? How dim can you make the bulb?

and a Rheostat

[FIGURE 13a]

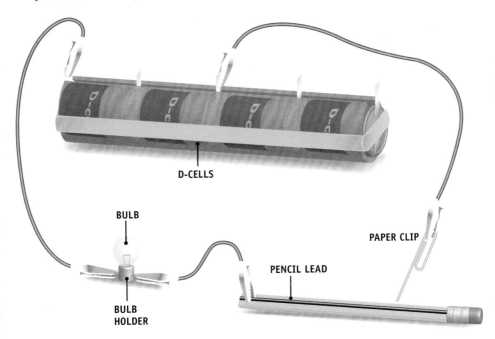

D-CELLS

BULB

BULB
HOLDER

PENCIL LEAD

PAPER CLIP

[FIGURE 13b]

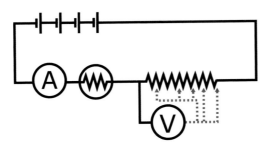

You can build a rheostat and measure its electrical resistance.

4. Use a battery, an ammeter, and a voltmeter to find out how the resistance of the pencil lead is related to its length (Figure 13b). Plot a graph of resistance, in ohms, versus length of the pencil lead in centimeters. What does the graph tell you?

Idea for a Science Fair Project

How do the resistances of different pencil leads (soft, medium, hard) compare? Is there any difference?

3.11 Electrical Resistance, a Short Circuit, and a Fuse

Things you will need:

- an adult
- safety goggles
- sink that is dry
- thin iron wire (such as a strand of picture hanging wire)
- insulated wires with clips
- 6-volt lantern battery

Do this experiment in a dry sink under close adult supervision. Wear safety goggles as a small flame may form.

In Experiment 3.3 you learned that connecting one pole of a battery to the other with a wire creates a short circuit. In this experiment you will create a short circuit on purpose.

1. Obtain a thin piece of iron wire about 4 cm (1.5 in) long.

2. Use an insulated wire with a clip to connect one end of the iron wire to one pole of a 6-volt lantern cell.

3. Use a second wire to connect the other end of the iron wire to the other pole of the battery. Watch closely. What happens?

   From what you saw in this experiment, why can short circuits be dangerous?

   Fuses are used to open a circuit that is carrying too much current. How did the iron wire act like a fuse?

3.12 Electrical Resistance

Things you will need:

- an adult
- measuring teaspoon
- 2 old teaspoons
- blue copper sulfate crystals $(CuSO_4 \cdot 5H_2O)$ (obtain from science teacher or a store that sells swimming pool supplies)
- drinking glass
- distilled or soft water
- insulated wires with clips
- ammeter, 0-5 A
- 6-volt lantern battery
- voltmeter, 0-6 V
- pen or pencil
- notebook

Many objects are covered with a thin layer of metal. The process used to do this is called plating. Jewelry is often gold plated. A thin layer of gold is spread over a less expensive metal.

In this experiment, you will plate an old spoon with copper. To do this you will need an electric current and a solution containing copper ions. Copper ions are copper atoms that carry a charge of +2 (Cu^{2+}).

1. **Put on plastic gloves and safety goggles and do this experiment under adult supervision.** Keep copper sulfate away from your mouth, hands, and eyes.

and Copper Plating

2. Add 2 or 3 teaspoons of blue copper sulfate crystals to half a glass of water. Stir to dissolve the crystals.

3. Place two old spoons on opposite sides of the glass. They will serve as electrodes. The positive electrode will be connected to the positive pole of the battery. Connect the other electrode to the negative pole of the battery.

4. Use insulated wires with clips to build a series circuit. The circuit will consist of the copper plating cell, an ammeter, and a 6-volt lantern battery (Figure 14). Add a voltmeter in parallel with the copper plating cell.

   What is the current through the copper plating cell? What is the voltage across the copper plating cell? What is the resistance of the copper plating cell? Does the resistance change as the process continues?

5. Wait a few minutes. You will see a thin orange layer of copper start to collect on one of the spoons. On which spoon is the copper collecting? Is the copper-coated spoon connected to the positive or the negative pole of the battery? Why do you think copper collects on one spoon and not the other?

[FIGURE 14]

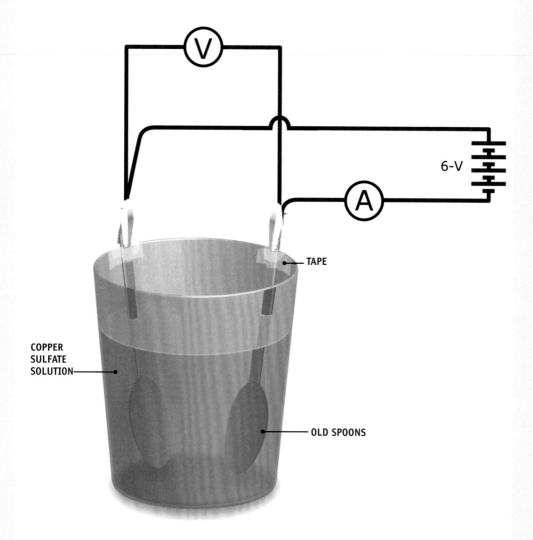

A copper plating experiment.

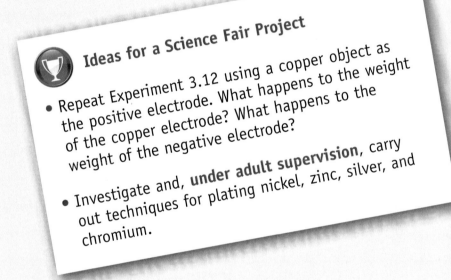

Ideas for a Science Fair Project

- Repeat Experiment 3.12 using a copper object as the positive electrode. What happens to the weight of the copper electrode? What happens to the weight of the negative electrode?

- Investigate and, **under adult supervision**, carry out techniques for plating nickel, zinc, silver, and chromium.

Compasses respond to the magnetic field around an electromagnet, just as they do to an ordinary magnet's field.

Chapter 4

Electricity and Magnetism: A Connection

FOR MANY YEARS, scientists felt there must be a connection between electricity and magnetism. There were positive and negative electric charges. Like charges repelled, unlike charges attracted. Magnets had north- and south-seeking poles. Like poles repelled, unlike poles attracted. Despite these similarities, magnets and electric charges seemed to have no effect on one another. Then, in 1819, Danish physicist Hans Christian Ørsted (1777–1851) discovered the connection. You can make the same discovery that Ørsted did nearly 200 years ago.

4.1 Ørsted's Discovery and

Things you will need:

- 1 or more magnetic compasses
- long insulated wire with connecting clips
- 4-D-cell battery
- long, straight piece of heavy copper wire
- cardboard box
- a partner
- 2 insulated wires with clips

1. Put a magnetic compass on a nonmetallic surface such as a wooden table.

2. Lay a long, straight insulated wire that has connecting clips at each end on the compass. Be sure that the wire is parallel to the compass needle (Figure 15a).

3. Connect one end of the wire to one electrode of a 2-D-cell battery. Briefly touch the other end of the wire to the other electrode. What happens to the compass needle?

4. Place the wire under the compass and repeat the experiment. What happens? What is the same? What is different?

5. Reverse the wire's connections to the battery. What happens? What does this tell you about the connection between an electric current and magnetism?

A week after Ørsted's discovery was published, André-Marie Ampère (1775–1836), a French physicist, devised a rule.

Ampère's Rule

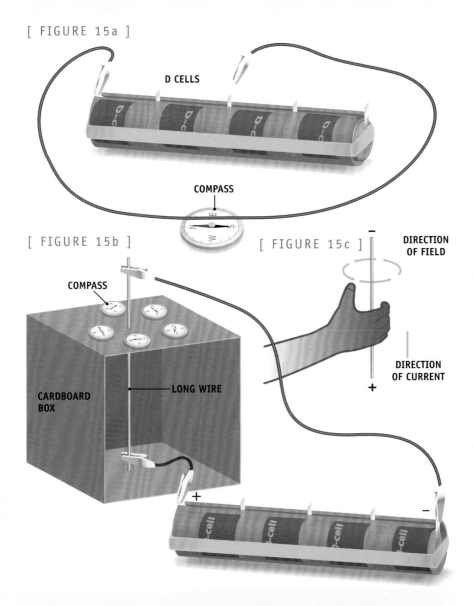

[FIGURE 15a]

D CELLS

COMPASS

[FIGURE 15b]

COMPASS

CARDBOARD
BOX

LONG WIRE

+

[FIGURE 15c]

–

DIRECTION
OF FIELD

DIRECTION
OF CURRENT

+

+

–

15a) What happens to a compass needle near an electric current?
  b) Mapping the magnetic field around an electric current.
  c) Ampère's right hand rule is shown here.

This rule enabled anyone to predict the direction of the magnetic field around an electric current. An experiment will show you how Ampère arrived at his rule.

6. Push a long, straight piece of heavy copper wire through one side of a cardboard box. See Figure 15b. If you have several magnetic compasses, place them around the wire as shown. (You could use iron filings rather than compasses.) If you only have one compass, ask a partner to slowly move the compass around the wire. Watch the compass as you do the next step.

7. Using insulated wires with clips, briefly connect the ends of the long wire to a 4-D-cell battery as shown. The connections form a short circuit so **it should not be connected for more than a few seconds**. As you can see, the magnetic field lines make a circular pattern around the electric current.

8. The direction of the field lines can be predicted by Ampère's "right hand rule." Point your right thumb in the direction positive charge would flow in the wire (+ to –). Your fingers curl in the direction of the magnetic field (S to N) around the wire. See Figure 15c. It shows the direction in which north-seeking poles would point. Do your results agree with this rule?

Direction of Electric Current

The direction of an electric current is defined as the direction that positive charge would flow—from a positive electrode to a negative electrode. This definition came from Benjamin Franklin. He thought of electricity as a fluid. It seemed reasonable that lots of fluid, which he called positive, would flow to less fluid, which he called negative. Today, we know that it is the negative charges (electrons) that actually move through wires.

4.2 Ampère, a Galvanometer, and Electric Meters

Things you will need:

- magnetic compass that has a transparent base and a scale marked in degrees (alternatively make a small protractor of your own that can be placed under a compass)
- scissors
- cardboard
- #24 enamel-coated wire
- sandpaper
- insulated wires with clips
- D-cell
- 6.3-volt flashlight bulb
- 2 100-ohm resistors

Ampère realized that the effect of an electric current on a compass needle could be used to measure current. A small protractor could be placed under the compass needle. A large turn of the needle would indicate a large current. A lesser turn would indicate a smaller current. You can build a galvanometer to see how this works.

1. Find a compass that has a transparent base and a scale marked in degrees. If you cannot find such a compass, draw a small protractor of your own on a small piece of paper. The protractor should be slightly larger than the compass. You can use it to measure the number of degrees that the needle moves.

2. Cut an "H" shape from a piece of cardboard. The compass should fit within the H as shown in Figure 16a.

3. Cut a piece of #24 enamel-coated wire approximately 2 meters (6.5 ft) long. Use a small piece of sandpaper to remove about 3 cm (1 in) of enamel from each end of the wire.

4. Wind the wire around the compass as shown in Figure 16b. Leave about 5 cm (2 in) at each end of the wire so you can make connections to other circuit elements.

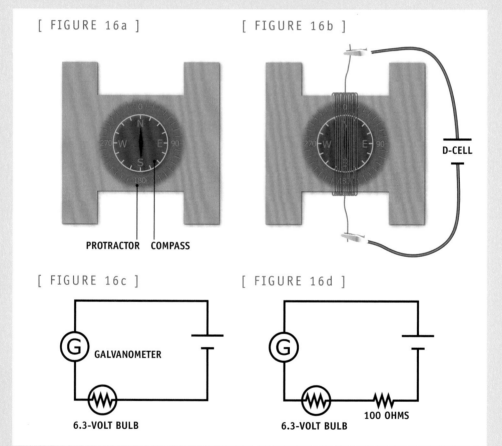

[FIGURE 16a]

[FIGURE 16b]

D-CELL

PROTRACTOR   COMPASS

[FIGURE 16c]

[FIGURE 16d]

GALVANOMETER

G

G

6.3-VOLT BULB

6.3-VOLT BULB

100 OHMS

16a) Make a platform for your galvanometer. b) Wrap wire around the compass parallel with the needle. c) Connect the galvanometer to a D-cell in series with a bulb. d) Add a 100-ohm resistor to the circuit.

5. Be sure the compass is turned so its needle points to 0 (zero) on the scale. Use two insulated wires with clips to connect the galvanometer to one D-cell. You have a short circuit so you will see the needle turn to 90 degrees (maximum deflection). Do not leave this circuit connected for more than a few seconds.

6. Place a 6.3-volt flashlight bulb in the circuit and connect it to the D-cell (Figure 16c). How much is the needle deflected when connected to the D-cell?

7. Add a 100-ohm (brown-black-brown) resistor to the series circuit (Figure 16d). How much is the needle deflected when connected to the D-cell? How much is the needle deflected if you add another 100-ohm resistor in series?

    Ammeters and voltmeters are more complex than the simple galvanometer you made. As you have seen, a voltmeter has a large resistor within it. An ammeter has practically no resistance. A spring restricts its motion.

Save your galvanometer for other experiments.

4.3 Ampère and Magnetic forces

Things you will need:
- thin aluminum foil
- scissors
- ruler
- tape
- wooden dowel
- table or counter
- long, flexible, insulated wires with clips
- 6-volt lantern battery

Ampère realized that parallel electric currents should exert forces on each other. The currents would produce magnetic fields. The magnetic fields would either push the wires together or apart. The direction of the force would depend on whether the currents were in the same or opposite directions. To see that this is true, you can do an experiment similar to Ampère's.

1. Cut a piece of thin aluminum foil about 75 cm (30 in) long and 1.2 cm (0.5 in) wide.

2. Tape a wooden dowel about 15 cm (6 in) long to the edge of a table or counter. See Figure 17a. Tape the two ends of the aluminum foil to opposite sides of the dowel as shown. Be sure the foil is not twisted as it hangs from the dowel. Be sure, too, that the sides of the foil are close together.

3. Clip a long, flexible, insulated wire to one end of the foil. Connect this wire to one pole of the 6-volt lantern battery.

4. Clip a similar wire to the other end of the foil. Notice that the current in the two sides of the loop will be in opposite directions.

on Side-by-Side Electric Currents

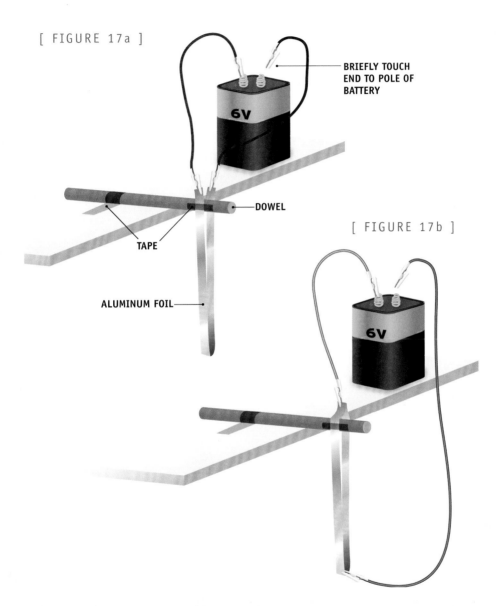

[FIGURE 17a]

BRIEFLY TOUCH
END TO POLE OF
BATTERY

6V

DOWEL

TAPE

ALUMINUM FOIL

[FIGURE 17b]

6V

17a) If currents flow in opposite directions, will parallel wires come together or move apart? b) If currents flow in the same direction, will parallel wires come together or move apart?

Be sure the foil is not moving. Watch the foil closely as you briefly touch the other end of this second wire to the other pole of the battery. Do the sides of the foil move closer together or farther apart?

5. Now make the current in both sides of the loop flow in the same direction. Join the two top ends of the foil by clipping a long, flexible, insulated wire to them. Clip the other end of this wire to one pole of the battery.

6. Clip another similar wire to the loop at the lower part of the foil (Figure 17b).

7. Be sure the foil is not moving and that the two sides of the foil are close together. Watch closely as you briefly touch the second wire to the other pole of the battery. Do the two sides of the foil move closer together or farther apart?

4.4 Magnets from Electric Currents

Things you will need:

- an adult
- about 15 meters (50 ft) of insulated copper wire
- empty cardboard cylinder from a roll of toilet paper
- wire stripper or knife
- 6-volt lantern battery
- magnetic compass
- 2 insulated wires with clips
- #24 enamel-coated copper wire
- sandpaper
- 2 D-cells
- wide rubber bands

Think about Ampère's right hand rule. A long coil of wire carrying an electric current should have a magnetic field similar to a bar magnet. You can do an experiment to see if this is true.

1. Obtain about 15 meters (50 ft) of insulated copper wire. Wind the wire around an empty cardboard cylinder from a roll of toilet paper. The length of the coil should be longer than the diameter.

2. **Ask an adult** to use a wire stripper or a knife to remove about 3 cm (1 in) of insulation from each end of the coil.

3. Use two insulated wires with clips to connect the ends of the coil to opposite poles of a 6-volt lantern battery. **Do not leave the coil connected for more than a few seconds!**

4. Move a compass slowly from one end of the coil to the other. Watch the compass needle as you do this. Is the magnetic field similar to the field around a bar magnet?

5. Think about the direction of the current in the coil (+ to –). Using the right hand rule, what should be the direction of the magnetic field inside the coil? Outside the coil? Does the field you predict agree with what the compass needle tells you?

6. Cut in half an 8 meter (26 ft) length of enamel coated wire. Make each half into a coil by wrapping the wire around a D-cell. Leave about 30 cm (1 ft) at each end of each wire uncoiled. Remove the coils from the D-cells. Use small pieces of tape to hold the wire coils in place.

7. Use sandpaper to remove the enamel from about 3 cm (1 in) of each end of the four straight (uncoiled) wires. These straight wires will be used to make connections to D-cells.

8. Attach the two leads from each coil to opposite poles of separate D-cells. Wide rubber bands can be used to hold the wires firmly against the D-cell poles. Do not leave the coils connected to the D-cells for very long or you will wear out the D-cells.

9. Predict what will happen if you bring the faces of these two coils close together while connected to D-cells. Can you make the coils attract one another? Can you make them repel one another?

4.5 An Electromagnet

Things you will need:
-paper clips
-large nail
-enameled copper wire
-sandpaper
-insulated wires with clips
-2 D-cells

In 1825, an English physicist, William Sturgeon (1783–1850), was the first to make a practical device from a magnet formed by a coil of wire. He varnished a soft iron rod. This insulated the iron from the bare copper wire he wrapped around it. The soft iron core dramatically increased the strength of the magnetic coil. The coil induced magnetism in the iron. Sturgeon was able to lift nine pounds of iron with his electromagnet, which weighed only a pound. Four years later, Joseph Henry (1797–1878), a teacher at Albany Academy in New York, made a much more powerful electromagnet. Henry used insulated wire. By so doing, he was able to wind many layers of wire around the iron core. Why was Sturgeon unable to make layers of coils? (See page 119 for an answer.)

In 1831, Henry supervised the construction of an electromagnet at Yale University. It lifted a ton of iron. This accomplishment earned him a position as a professor at Princeton University.

You can easily make an electromagnet.

1. Try to lift a paper clip by touching it with a large unmagnetized nail.

2. Enclose part of the nail in a wire coil by winding a hundred turns of enameled copper wire around the nail. Always wrap in the same direction. Leave about 30 cm (1 ft) of wire at each end of the coil.

3. Use sandpaper to remove about 3 cm (1 in) of the enamel from each end of the wire.

4 Using insulated wires with clips, connect the ends of the coil to opposite poles of a D-cell. Do not leave the wires connected for very long or you will wear out the D-cell.

5. How many end-to-end paper clips can you lift with your electromagnet? What happens when you disconnect the coil from the D-cell?

6 Remove fifty of the hundred turns of wire you used to make the coil. How many paper clips can your electromagnet lift now? How does the number of turns in the coil affect the strength of your electromagnet?

7. Connect the electromagnet to a 2-D-cell battery. How many paper clips can your electromagnet lift now? How does the number of D-cells connected to the electromagnet affect its strength?

8. Prepare another electromagnet. Wrap half the coils clockwise and the other half counterclockwise. What is the strength of this electromagnet. Can you explain why?

 Ideas for a Science Fair Project

- Do an experiment to find out if the size of the iron core affects the strength of an electromagnet.

- Try cores other than iron, such as pencil leads, aluminum, copper, lead, glass, plastic, and so on. Do any of them improve the electromagnetic strength of the wire coil?

🏆 4.6 Conductors and Nonconductors

Things you will need:

- things to test: metal items such as coins, nails, paper clips; plastic items; wooden items; paper; wax; chalk; liquids such as water, salt water, sugar water, vinegar, household ammonia, and oil

- 6.3-volt bulb
- 4-D-cell battery
- insulated wires with clips
- paper clips
- plastic medicine cup or vial
- galvanometer you built in Experiment 4.2

Some things (conductors) conduct an electric current. Some things (nonconductors or insulators) do not. You can find out which things are conductors and which are nonconductors.

1. Set up the circuit shown in Figure 18a. Test the solid items you have collected, in turn, with one, two, three, and four D-cells. If the bulb lights, you can be sure you have a conductor. Make a list of conductors and nonconductors.

2. To test liquids, slip paper clips over opposite sides of a plastic medicine cup or vial. See Figure 18b. Half of each paper clip should be inside the cup or vial. Pour a liquid to be tested into the cup or vial. The liquid should cover as much of the paper

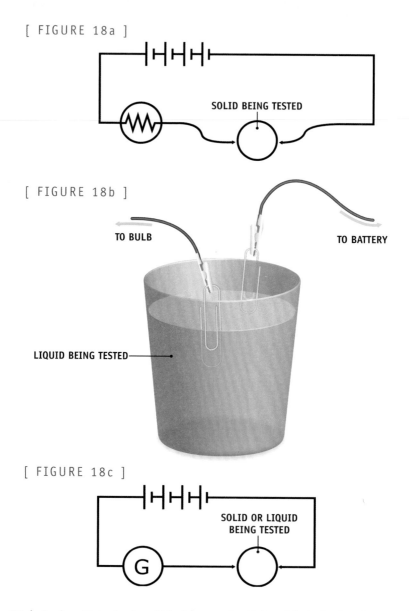

[FIGURE 18a]

SOLID BEING TESTED

[FIGURE 18b]

TO BULB

TO BATTERY

LIQUID BEING TESTED

[FIGURE 18c]

SOLID OR LIQUID
BEING TESTED

G

18a) A circuit to test solids for conductivity. b) A device for testing
liquids for conductivity. c) A way to separate poor conductors
from nonconductors.

clip inside the vial as possible. Connect the paper clip electrodes to the bulb as you did with the solid items. Which liquids seem to be conductors? Which are nonconductors?

In some of the liquids you tested, you may have seen small bubbles around the electrodes. This suggests electric currents too small to light the bulb. You can retest questionable items with a more sensitive indicator.

3. Replace the bulb with your galvanometer (Figure 18c).

4. Retest items that you think may be poor conductors but not nonconductors. Are there nonconductors that you will now classify as poor conductors?

Ideas for a Science Fair Project

• Find out which parts of a flashlight bulb are conductors and which are nonconductors. Do the same for a D-cell. How do your results help explain what you found in Experiment 3.3?

• Ask an adult to help you take a bulb apart. Can you see the connections that must be made to make the bulb conduct electric current?

4.1 Curie Point

The French chemist Pierre Curie (1859–1906) studied magnetism. He discovered that magnetic materials, such as iron, cobalt, and nickel, lose their magnetism at specific temperatures. The temperature at which a magnetic material loses its magnetism is called the Curie point *in his honor. Pierre and his wife, Marie Curie (1867–1934), also did extensive research with radioactive materials. Marie received two Nobel prizes, in physics and chemistry, for her work.*

To see that magnetic materials lose their magnetism at a high temperature, you can do an experiment. Do it under adult supervision *because you will be producing very high temperatures.*

1. Cut a piece of thin iron wire about 8 cm (3 in) long.

2. Support the wire by using small pieces of duct tape to attach it to two upright popsicle sticks. Let about 1.3 cm (0.5 in) of wire extend beyond each stick. Lumps of clay can be used to keep the

sticks upright as shown in Figure 19. Attach the alligator clips of two insulated wires to the ends of the iron wire as shown.

3. Hang a small magnet from a thread. The upper end of the thread can be taped to a beam, a counter or table top, an overhead light's string switch, or some similar support. The magnet should be free to swing like a pendulum.

4. Pull the magnet to one side and touch it to the center of the iron wire as shown. It should stick to the wire. But it should not touch either alligator clip outside the popsicle sticks.

5. Connect the other ends of the insulated wires to the poles of the lantern battery as shown (Figure 19). The iron wire will get very hot. As soon as the magnet swings away from the wire, disconnect the battery.

What happened to the magnetic property of the iron wire? Why do you think it happened?

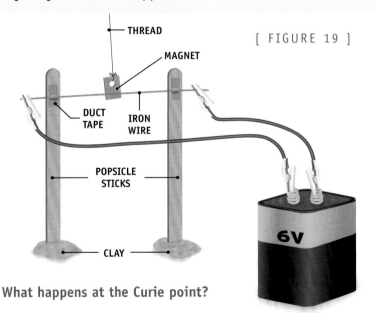

[FIGURE 19]

THREAD

MAGNET

DUCT TAPE

IRON WIRE

POPSICLE STICKS

6V

CLAY

What happens at the Curie point?

An electric motor, seen here, works by passing an electric current through a changing magnetic field. The change in the magnetic field causes the wire inside the motor, which is carrying the current, to spin, generating motion.

Chapter 5

Faraday, Electric Motors, and Generators

MICHAEL FARADAY (1791–1867) was a self-taught English physicist and chemist. He built the world's first electric motor and generator. Faraday was one of ten children born to a working-class family. His father was a blacksmith. In those days, education was not available to working-class people. Instead, Faraday went to work for a bookbinder. This was a fortunate decision. It enabled young Michael to read a great many books. Luckily for civilization, his boss encouraged Faraday to attend scientific lectures as well.

Following a lecture by Humphry Davy (1778–1829), a great English chemist, Faraday was very excited. He sent Davy a copy of the notes he had taken along with drawings. Davy was impressed. He hired Faraday as his assistant. Faraday accepted the position even though it meant a decrease in salary. From that point on, until his retirement, Faraday spent most of his life in the laboratory. His discoveries led to the worldwide use of electrical energy. He retired several years before his death because of failing memory. His memory losses were probably caused by exposure to mercury vapors in his laboratory.

5.1 The Motor Principle: The force

Things you will need:
- 6 square or round ceramic magnets or a strong horseshoe magnet
- wire cutter
- about 60 cm (2 ft) of flexible 20-gauge magnet wire (enamel-coated copper wire)
- sandpaper
- tape
- cardboard
- 2 insulated wires with clips
- D-cell

In Chapter 4 you learned of Ørsted's discovery—the connection between electricity and magnetism. A year later, Faraday made the world's first electric motor. His motor consisted of magnets and wires rotating in cups of mercury. Since mercury is poisonous, you should not duplicate Faraday's experiment. However, you can observe the basic principle behind all electric motors.

1. Obtain six square or round ceramic magnets. Join them together so their opposite poles attract. Separate them in the middle so there is a north pole on one side of the gap and a south pole on the other side.

2. Tape them to a sheet of cardboard so that the gap is about 1.3 cm (0.5 in) wide (Figure 20a). (If you have a strong horseshoe magnet, see Figure 20b.)

3   Cut a piece of flexible magnet wire (enamel coated copper wire) about 60 cm (2 ft) long. Remove about 3 cm (1 in) of insulation (enamel) from each end of the wire.

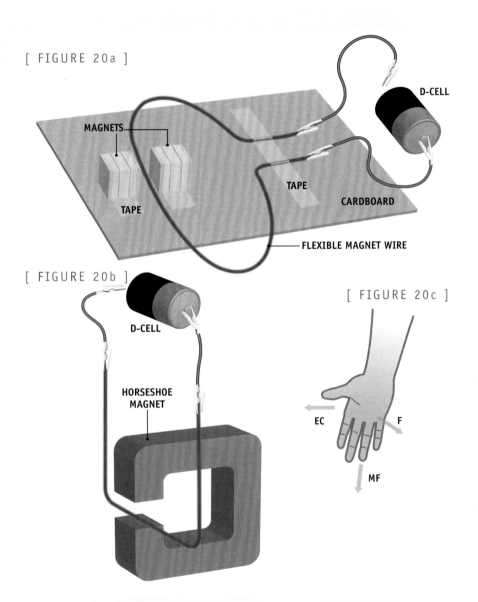

[FIGURE 20a]

MAGNETS

D-CELL

TAPE

TAPE

CARDBOARD

FLEXIBLE MAGNET WIRE

[FIGURE 20b]

D-CELL

HORSESHOE
MAGNET

[FIGURE 20c]

EC

F

MF

20a) Demonstrating the motor principle using ceramic magnets.
  b) Demonstrating the motor principle using a horseshoe magnet.
  c) The right hand rule: EC = electric current; MF = magnetic field;
     F = force on current in the wire.

4. Tape the parts of the wire near their ends to the cardboard as shown. Be sure the straight portion of the wire lies between the centers of the magnet's poles. It should be off the surface and about half as high as the height of the magnets. Attach the clips of two insulated wires to the ends of the flexible magnet wire. Attach the other end of one of those wires to one pole of a D-cell.

5. Watch the wire between the magnets as you touch the end of the second insulated wire to the other pole of the D-cell. What happens?

6. Turn the D-cell around to reverse the current in the wire. Repeat the experiment. What happens this time?

7. You can predict the direction the wire will be pushed. You will have to use another right hand rule. (See Figure 20c.) Turn your thumb so it is perpendicular to your index finger, but in the same plane as your palm. Now point your thumb in the direction of the electric current in the wire (the direction positive charge would move). Point your fingers in the direction of the magnetic field (N pole to S pole). Your palm, as you would use it to push something, will give the direction the wire will be pushed.

   Electric motors work on the basis of this simple principle. A coil of wire carries a current perpendicular to the field created by magnets inside the motor. The magnetic force on the coil causes it to turn. In the next experiment, you will build a simple electric motor.

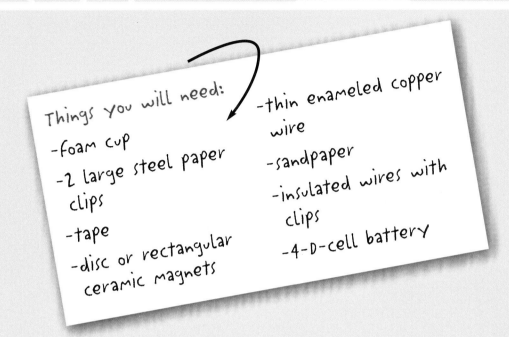

Things you will need:
- foam cup
- 2 large steel paper clips
- tape
- disc or rectangular ceramic magnets
- thin enameled copper wire
- sandpaper
- insulated wires with clips
- 4-D-cell battery

1. Turn a foam cup upside down.

2. Obtain two large steel paper clips. Unfold one end of each (Figure 21). Tape them to opposite sides of the foam cup.

3. Put two disc or square ceramic magnets on top of the cup. Put a third magnet inside the cup directly under the others.

4. Wind about 30 cm (1 ft) of enameled copper wire around your first two fingers. Leave about 5 cm (2 in) of wire at each end of the coil you have made.

5. Wrap these ends around opposite sides of the coil several times. This will help keep the wires in place. Use two small pieces of tape to hold the coil together.

6. Straighten the ends that stick out from opposite sides of the coil. Use sandpaper to remove the enamel from these ends.

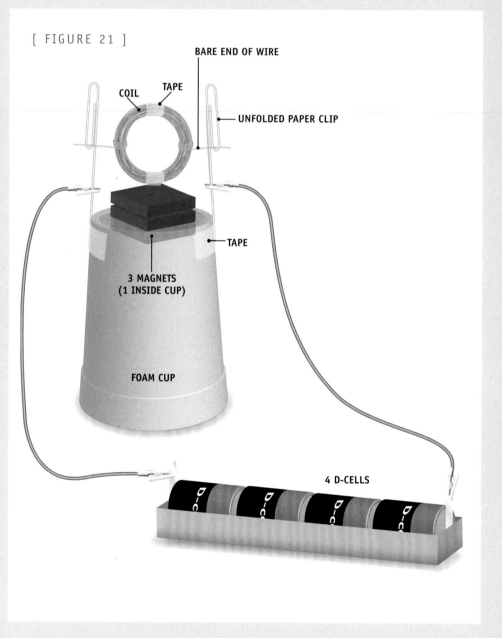

[FIGURE 21]

BARE END OF WIRE

COIL   TAPE

UNFOLDED PAPER CLIP

TAPE

3 MAGNETS
(1 INSIDE CUP)

FOAM CUP

4 D-CELLS

You can build a simple DC motor.

7. Put the sandpapered ends of the coil into the loops formed by the paper clips. Gently turn the coil. It should come very close to the top of the magnet.

8. Use wires with clips to connect the poles of a 4-D-cell battery to the paper clips. Give the coil a gentle flip and watch it spin. Do not leave the battery connected for more than a few seconds.

    Will the motor work with fewer D-cells? With fewer magnets? Will increasing the length of wire used in the coil have any effect? Will an additional magnet have any effect on the motor?

Ideas for a Science Fair Project

- Direct-current (DC) motors (those that connect to a battery) require a commutator to work properly. Your motor had no commutator. Find out how a commutator works. Then explain why your motor works without one.

- Build a DC motor that includes a commutator.

- Use a small electric motor and electric cells to build a toy electric car.

- Use a small electric motor and three D-cells to build a three-speed fan.

5.3 Electricity from Magnets:

Things you will need:
- enameled wire
- large nail
- sandpaper
- insulated wires with clips
- microammeter
- 6-volt lantern battery
- bar magnet
- galvanometer you made in Experiment 4.2
- plastic tube or bottle about 2 inches in diameter
- clay

Faraday knew that moving charges produce a magnetic field. He knew, too, that a current in a coil acts like a bar magnet. He reasoned it should be possible to produce an electric current using magnets. He tried placing large magnets near coils of wire, but no currents were induced. Then, on December 25, 1831, he made a discovery. (Actually, Joseph Henry made the discovery before Faraday, but Henry did not publish his results until after Faraday did.) You can make the same discovery by doing an experiment similar to Faraday's.

1. Wind a hundred turns of enameled wire around one half of a large nail. Always wrap in the same direction. Leave about 30 cm (1 ft) of wire at each end of the coil. Use sandpaper to remove about 3 cm (1 in) of the insulating enamel from each end of the wire.

Electromagnetic Induction

2. Wind a similar coil around the other half of the nail. Sandpaper its ends as well.

3. Using wires with clips, connect the ends of one coil to the poles of a microammeter.

4. Use a wire with clips to connect one end of the other coil to one pole of a lantern battery. Connect another wire with clips to the other end of that coil. Watch the meter as you touch the other end of this wire to the other pole of the battery. What happens to the meter? What happens when you disconnect the battery? You have observed what Faraday saw almost 200 years ago.

Faraday was also famous for his public lectures and demonstrations. He did a simple demonstration for his audience. It showed that an electric current is generated *only when a magnetic field through a coil is changing*. You can do the same demonstration.

5. Move a bar magnet about 30 cm (1 ft) from the galvanometer you made in Experiment 4.2. You will see the compass needle move. Move the magnet farther from the galvanometer until its movement has no effect on the compass needle.

6. At that distance, use enamel coated wire to make a coil. Wrap fifty windings around a plastic tube or bottle that is about 5 cm (2 in) in diameter. Sandpaper the ends of the coil. Remove the coil. Tape the coiled wire together. Use a lump of clay to keep the coil upright.

7. Use long insulated wires with clips to connect the galvanometer to the coil.

8. Move a bar magnet into the coil. What happens to the galvanometer? Pull the magnet out of the coil. What happens to the galvanometer? What happens when the magnet is not moving?

   How does the rate at which you move the magnet affect the current that is induced?

   How do you think Faraday explained this demonstration to his audience? How would you explain it?

🏆 5.4 A Motor as a Generator

Things you will need:

- <u>an adult</u>
- toy electric motor (obtain from a hobby shop, toy store, or science supply company)
- 2 insulated wires with clips
- milli- or microammeter
- bicycle
- gloves
- 1.2-volt flashlight bulb
- bulb holder

You now know how an electric motor works. Electric charges are pushed perpendicular to a magnetic field when they move. The push causes a coil to turn. The coil is connected to a shaft. When the coil turns, so does the shaft. The turning shaft can do work.

Suppose you or some other force turns the shaft. This will cause the coil to turn in a magnetic field. The strength of the magnetic field through the coil will change. The change will induce a current in the coil. If you turn the shaft of the motor, it should become an electric generator.

1. The two small metal leads from a toy electric motor are connected to the motor's coil. Use two insulated wires with clips to connect those two leads to the poles of a milli- or microammeter.

2. Turn the motor's shaft with your fingers. Is an electric current generated? What happens if you turn the shaft faster? Can you explain why it happens?

3. Turn a bicycle upside down. Give the front wheel a spin. **Ask an adult** wearing a glove to hold the motor's shaft against the side of the spinning tire. Can a reasonably steady current be generated as the wheel spins?

4. Connect the motor's leads to a 1.2-volt flashlight bulb in a bulb holder. Again, **ask an adult** wearing a glove to hold the motor's shaft against the side of a spinning bike tire. Can enough current be generated to light the bulb?

Generating Electricity

For safety reasons, the experiments in this book use electric cells or batteries as the source of electric current and voltage. However, most electricity is generated the way your toy motor produced it. In electric power plants, huge wire coils inside giant magnets are turned by large machines called turbines. The turbines are made to spin by flowing water or by steam.

Idea for a Science Fair Project

Figure out a way to use water power to generate a steady electric current from your toy motor. This is the way electricity is generated in a hydroelectric power station.

These power plants generate an alternating current (AC). The batteries you used produce a direct current (DC). Alternating currents, found in the electricity in your home, switch direction sixty times per second (60 hertz). The voltage across home appliances, such as refrigerators, light bulbs, radios, and so on, must also alternate at 60 Hz. The voltage varies from 0 to 170 volts. The average voltage is approximately 120 volts. This is twenty times the highest voltage you used in your experiments.

Considerable engineering and thought went into the development of the generators that produce electricity. However, the basic principle on which they operate was discovered by Michael Faraday. Similarly, the electric motors found in so many places operate on the principle discovered by Faraday.

Things you will need:
- *electric meter*
- *pen or pencil*
- *notebook*
- *pocket calculator (optional)*
- *electric bill*
- *wattage ratings of appliances*

At the point where electric power lines enter your home, there is a meter. There may be a meter like the one in Figure 22. To read the meter shown in Figure 22, start from the left. The meter reads 51,138. (Why is the number in the tens place 3 and not 4?) Your power company reads your meter each month to determine your family's electric bill. The meter measures electric energy in kilowatt-hours (kWh). They might charge you ten cents for each kilowatt-hour of electrical energy. To see how they determine their monthly charge, read one of their monthly bills.

1. Find out when the power company reads your family's electric meter. Make and record your own readings at about the same time.

2. Calculate the number of kilowatt-hours the power company supplied your home for that month. Does your calculation agree closely with theirs?

3. The wattage rating of most electrical appliances can be found somewhere on the appliance. A kilowatt (kW) is 1,000 watts (1 kW = 1,000 W). A toaster might have a wattage rating of 750 W, which is 0.75 kW. If the toaster is operated for one hour, the energy required is 0.75 kW × 1 h = 0.75 kWh.

4. Find the wattage ratings for a number of appliances in your home.

5. Calculate the energy in kilowatt-hours to operate each appliance for one hour.

[FIGURE 22]

An example of an electric meter used by electric companies.

6. Estimate the number of hours each appliance is used during a year. Then estimate the cost to operate each appliance for one year.

An Ending Thought to Consider

When George Washington was president, generating electricity other than with batteries was unknown. How did people live without electricity? How did they light their homes? Cool and preserve their food? Wash their clothes? Obtain their news? Carry out the many other activities for which we use electricity?

ANSWERS TO QUESTIONS

Experiment 2.3

• The north seeking pole of a compass or magnet is attracted to Earth's magnetic pole in Boothia Bay; therefore, that magnetic pole must be a south-seeking pole.

• In Boothia Bay, Canada, the compass needle would point straight down above Earth's south-seeking pole.

• In Antarctica the compass needle would point straight up above Earth's north-seeking pole.

Experiment 2.5

It would turn upward at Earth's north-seeking pole in Antarctica. The compass needle's north-seeking pole would be pointing straight up. You might say it has a negative dip of 90 degrees.

Experiment 3.3

The bulbs will light in circuits b, c, and h. Circuits a, d, and e are short circuits. Bulbs in circuits f and g are connected to only one pole of the D-cell.

Electrical Resistance and Georg Simon Ohm: The resistance of a wire increases with temperature. As the voltage increased, more current flowed through the bulb's filament. It became brighter and warmer. As the filament became hotter, its resistance increased.

Experiment 4.5

Sturgeon used bare wire. If he had tried to wrap a second layer, he would have created a short circuit.

APPENDIX:
SCIENCE SUPPLY COMPANIES

Arbor Scientific
P.O. Box 2750
Ann Arbor, MI 48106-2750
(800) 367-6695
www.arborsci.com

Carolina Biological Supply Co.
2700 York Road
Burlington, NC 27215-3398
(800) 334-5551
www.carolina.com

**Connecticut Valley Biological
Supply Co., Inc.**
82 Valley Road, Box 326
Southampton, MA 01073
(800) 628-7748
www.ctvalleybio.com

Delta Education
P.O. Box 3000
80 Northwest Blvd
Nashua, NH 03061-3000
(800) 258-1302
customerservice@delta-education.com

Edmund Scientific's Scientifics
60 Pearce Avenue
Tonawanda, NY 14150-6711
(800) 728-6999
www.scientificsonline.com

Educational Innovations, Inc.
362 Main Avenue
Norwalk, CT 06851
(888) 912-7474
www.teachersource.com

Fisher Science Education
4500 Turnberry
Hanover Park, IL 60133
(800) 955-1177
www.fisheredu.com

Frey Scientific
100 Paragon Parkway
Mansfield, OH 44903
(800) 225-3739
www.freyscientific.com

Nasco-Fort Atkinson
P.O. Box 901
Fort Atkinson, WI 53538-0901
(800) 558-9595
www.enasco.com/science

Nasco-Modesto
P.O. Box 3837
Modesto, CA 95352-3837
(800) 558-9595
www.enasco.com/science

Sargent-Welch/VWR Scientific
P.O. Box 5229
Buffalo Grove, IL 60089-5229
(800) SAR-GENT
www.SargentWelch.com

Science Kit & Boreal Laboratories
777 East Park Drive
P.O. Box 5003
Tonawanda, NY 14150
(800) 828-7777
www.sciencekit.com

Wards Natural Science Establishment
P.O. Box 92912
Rochester, NY 14692-9012
(800) 962-2660

GLOSSARY

ammeter—An instrument (meter) used to measure electric current.

ampere—A unit of electric current. One ampere is a flow of charge equal to one coulomb per second or 6.25 billion billion electrons per second.

battery—A number of electric cells joined in series or in parallel.

coulomb—A unit of charge equal to 6.25 billion billion electrons.

current electricity—The science of electric charges that are moving.

D-cell—An electric cell that has a carbon rod (the positive electrode) and an electrolyte of powdered carbon mixed with manganese dioxide, ammonium chloride, and water. The entire cell is enclosed in a zinc can that serves as the negative electrode.

electric cell—Sometimes incorrectly called a battery, it consists of two electrodes made of different metals placed in an electrolyte. When connected to a circuit, chemical reactions in the cell create a voltage that can cause charges to flow through the circuit.

electric current—A flow of electric charge.

electrical resistance—The ratio of the voltage across an element in an electric circuit to the current flowing through it.

electricity—The science of electrically charged objects.

electroscope—A device used to detect electric charge.

fuse—A circuit element with little resistance that will melt if a large current flows through it.

galvanometer—An instrument that can detect and measure an electric current.

magnet—An object that attracts iron and certain other materials. It can both attract and repel another magnet.

magnetic compass—A small magnet that is free to turn. It can be used to find directions or to map a magnetic field.

magnetic matter—Matter that can be magnetized so that it is attracted to a magnet, but is not itself a magnet. It is attracted to either pole of a magnet. Once the attracting magnet is removed, the matter does not behave like a true magnet.

negative charge—The charge on a rubber rod rubbed with fur.

nonmagnetic matter—Matter that is neither attracted nor repelled by a magnet.

ohm—A unit of electrical resistance. One ohm equals one volt per ampere.

parallel circuit—A circuit consisting of two or more circuit elements, such as light bulbs, connected side-by-side so that an electric current divides as it passes through the circuit.

positive charge—The charge on a glass rod rubbed with silk.

resistor—A circuit element that is used to reduce electric current because it resists the flow of electric charges.

rheostat—A circuit element that allows you to vary the circuit's resistance.

series circuit—A circuit consisting of two or more circuit elements, such as light bulbs, connected one after the other.

short circuit—A circuit in which a battery's positive pole is connected directly to its negative pole with no circuit elements other than the connecting wire. Such a circuit becomes very hot.

static electricity—The science of electric charges that are not moving.

volt—A unit used to measure the energy carried by a coulomb of electric charge. One volt is equal to one joule of energy per coulomb of charge.

voltmeter—An instrument (meter) used to measure voltage.

FURTHER READING

Books

Bardhan-Quallen, Sudipta, *Championship Science Fair Projects: 100 Sure-to-Win Experiments*. New York: Sterling, 2004.

Bartholomew, Alan. *Electric Mischief: Battery-Powered Gadgets Kids Can Build*. Toronto: Kids Can Press, 2002.

Bochinski, Julianne Blair. *More Award-Winning Science Fair Projects*. Hoboken, N.J.: John Wiley and Sons, 2004.

Cheshire, Gerard. *Electricity and Magnetism*. North Mankato, Minn.: Smart Apple Media, 2007.

Dispezio, Michael A. *Super Sensational Science Fair Projects*. New York: Sterling Publishers, 2002.

Dreier, David. *Electrical Circuits: Harnessing Electricity*. Minneapolis: Compass Point Books, 2008.

Gardner, Robert. *Electricity and Magnetism Science Fair Projects Using Batteries, Balloons, and Other Hair-Raising Stuff*. Berkeley Heights, N.J.: Enslow Publishers, Inc., 2004.

Lauw, Darlene, and Lim Cheng Puay. *Electricity*. New York: Crabtree Publishing Company, 2002.

Rhadigan, Joe, and Rain Newcomb. *Prize-Winning Science Fair Projects for Curious Kids*. New York: Lark Books, 2004.

Tocci, Salvatore. *Experiments with Electricity*. New York: Children's Press, 2002.

FURTHER READING

Internet Addresses

Electronics for Kids

users.stargate.net/~eit/kidspage.htm

Electricity Unit

wow.osu.edu/experiments/electricity/eleclist.html

Electricity and Magnetism Lessons from Scouting Resources

www.scoutingresources.org.uk/badge_scienceexp05.html

INDEX

P

parallel circuits, 62–64, 90–92
Peregrinus, Petrus, 27
plating, 78–81
poles
    Earth's, 34–36
    magnetic, 37–39
    notation, 59
    overview, 28–29
    in short circuits, 56, 57, 77

R

repelling forces, 16–19, 21
resistance. *See* electrical resistors.
rheostats (dimmer switches),
    74–76
right hand rule, 84–86, 93–95,
    105, 106

S

safety, 8–9
science fairs, 7–8
scientific method, 10–11
series circuits, 62–64, 79, 80
short circuits, 56, 57, 77, 86, 89

static electricity
    Benjamin Franklin and, 17–19
    William Gilbert and, 14–16
    nerves and, 47
Sturgeon, William, 95

T

temperature
    current flow and, 72
    magnetism and, 100–101
Thales of Miletus, 13, 27
turbines, 114

V

versorium, 14–16
Volta, Alessandro, 47
voltage graphs, 60, 70
voltaic pile, 48–51
voltmeters, 49, 59, 73, 89

W

water
    as coolant, 68, 69
    electrical attraction of, 21
wattage of appliances, 115–118

About the Author

Robert Gardner is an award-winning author of science books for young readers. He retired from Salisbury School in Connecticut, where he chaired the science department for more than 30 years, to pursue a career as an author. He lives on Cape Cod with his wife, Patsy, and enjoys writing, biking, and doing volunteer work.